"A GREAT BOOK! People turn to a chapter, find a suggestion or a technique that seems to apply, try it, and it usually helps. The book is very readable and the instructions for the techniques are so clear that people can follow them easily. A terrific self-help book — A REAL CONTRIBUTION!"

-John Garrison, Ph.D.
Clinical Psychologist
Department of Behavioral Medicine
Atlanticare Medical Center
Lynn, Massachusetts

"A GEM OF A BOOK!" Straight-forward, usable. Its many concrete examples add greatly to its value."

-A. Harvey Baker, Ph.D.
Professor of Psychology
Queens College
New York, New York

"*Stress? Find Your Balance* contains an excellent sample of stress-management procedures for our patients to start with to find out what works best for them. People really benefit from the book's encouraging them to customize their own programs. Our patients often bring the book with them — I've seen their copies become more and more dog-eared with time. People not only like this book, they use it well."

-Erik Laur
Biofeedback Therapist
Department of Behavioral Medicine
St. Anthony's Hospital
Amarillo, Texas

"In one brief and very readable volume, Osterkamp and Press have managed to distill the very essence of the stress-management literature. *Stress? Find Your Balance* covers the central threads of stress management so well, I refer to it as 'the Cliffs Notes of stress management.' I have found this book to be an invaluable tool in working in a stress counseling role. People of virtually all levels of stress and all walks of life can find something of value — which they use!"

-Frank J. Gilbert, Ph.D.
Wellness Coordinator
WELLPLAN—Salina Family Physicians
Salina, Kansas

"Contains a multitude of helpful stress-fighting strategies presented in an understandable and concise fashion. My clients find it brief enough to read while at the same time comprehensive enough to be of value. A commendable contribution to stress-management training!"

-Craig S. Brown, Ed.D.
Licensed Psychologist
Jackson, Michigan

"I've found *Stress? Find Your Balance* to be valuable and effective in helping clients in my private practice to reduce their stress. Perhaps the most significant aspect of the book is the way it helps people deal with change by answering the ultimate question, 'How?' "

-Milton A. Rubin, Ph.D.
Licensed Psychologist
Behavioral Psychological Services,
St. Louis, Missouri

STRESS?

FIND YOUR BALANCE

by

Lynn Osterkamp, Ph.D.

and

Allan N. Press, Ph.D.

Second Edition • 1988

PREVENTIVE MEASURES, INC.

LAWRENCE, KANSAS

First edition published 1983 by Celestial Express, Lakewood, Colorado.

Second Edition published by:
Preventive Measures, Inc.
1115 West Campus Road
Lawrence, Kansas, 66044.

Cover Design by Kim Farrer.

Printed in the United States of America.

First edition: 1983	10,000 copies
Second edition:	
First Printing: May, 1988	10,000 copies
Second Printing, January, 1989	10,000 copies

The personal stories in this book are true, but all names and all identifying characteristics of the individuals mentioned have been changed inorder to protect their privacy.

Library of Congress Catalog Card Number: 83-73013

International Standard Book Number: 0-9620725-0-8

Dedicated to

Laurel, Jeffrey, and Barbara

Acknowledgments

We gratefully acknowledge the many health and mental health professionals around the country who have enthusiastically recommended the first edition of this book to their patients and clients, and who have encouraged us to publish this revised edition.

We also appreciate the technical advice, assistance, and unfailing good humor of Pat Emerson, who made it possible for us to produce the entire book through computerized typesetting.

CONTENTS

II. TECHNIQUES THAT MAKE YOU FEEL BETTER AND MAKE YOUR LOAD EASIER TO CARRY

PREFACE TO THE REVISED EDITION

Somehow this book seems to be always growing and changing. It began in the mid-1970's as a series of handouts for participants in our stress-management workshops. Later we revised, expanded and compiled the handouts into a pamphlet—the first *Stress? Find Your Balance*. We gave out the pamphlet in our workshops and classes; people read it, tried its suggestions, and lent it to friends, relatives and clients. Soon we began getting inquiries from people around the country who had seen the pamphlet and wanted to buy extra copies.

By that time we had assembled a large collection of personal reports from our students and clients who had been using the stress-management techniques to change their lives. We found reading their descriptions to be inspiring, encouraging and always entertaining. So we decided to expand and revise our pamphlet into a book that would include many of these personal examples (with names and identifying characteristics changed to preserve their anonymity). That book was published in 1983 by a new press, Celestial Express of Lakewood Colorado. We continued to use the book in our workshops and classes through an agreement with Celestial Express that allowed us to purchase copies inexpensively.

Meanwhile we had begun developing our *Computerized Stress Inventory* (*CSI*), a comprehensive computerized stress assessment that would give people an analysis of their strengths and weaknesses plus suggestions for positive lifestyle change. Again, it was a project that we started for our own use, because we needed it for our work—and again it grew beyond our expectations. Our research, programming, testing and retesting resulted in the original *CSI*, published in 1984. Part of our field testing of the *CSI* was done through the Wellife Program at the Lawrence Family Practice Center. Their staff, to whom we will always be grateful, convinced us to combine the book with the assessment by including references to specific book chapters in individuals' *CSI Reports*— references that instructed people to read certain chapters that would help them cope with areas of high stress in their lives.

This package of stress-management book and individualized assessment has proven to be such an effective teaching tool that it is now used by health and mental health professionals in clinics, private practices, corporations, wellness and fitness centers, universities, military installations and other settings nationwide and in several foreign countries. We formed our own company, *Preventive Measures, Inc.* to market and distributute the *CSI*, which we have expanded to include a Brief as well as a Comprehensive version in a paper-and-pencil as well as a computerized format. We have continued our own research and teaching in this growing field of stress-management, part of which involves maintaining a large database of responses to the *CSI*.

Eventually we bought back from Celestial Express their entire stock of *Stress? Find Your Balance,* as well as all publishing rights, so that we could more easily distribute the combined book and assessment package. We have not marketed this book in bookstores; instead we sell it to health and mental health professionals who distribute it to their patients and clients. Their overwhelming enthusiasm continues to support our confidence in the effectiveness of the simple techniques and positive philosophy we teach. Personal reports from our own students and clients constantly expand and reinforce our beliefs about people's enormous capacity for making positive change in their lives. We very much appreciate their generosity in sharing their experiences.

Demand for the book continues to grow through the professional grapevine and from readers who want extra copies to replace ones they "loaned out" or to give to friends and relatives. We are pleased because we know from long personal experience that the techniques we present here do work, and we want to promote their use as widely as possible.

We see this revised edition of *Stress? Find Your Balance* as yet another step in the process. We have updated and expanded the material, and have included even more personal examples that show how people actually use the techniques. For us, the revisions have been a pleasant way of "renewing our acquaintance" with former students and clients as we sifted through boxes of their progress reports. We hope you, our readers, will enjoy and benefit from their experiences as much as we have, and will be inspired by their successes to pursue your own program of change.

A.N.P. & L.O.
April, 1988

SECTION I :
THE QUESTIONS

1. Do You Feel Like You're Carrying A Heavy Load ....
   And Sometimes It's Just Too Much?

2. What Is The Load ....
   And Why Is It So Heavy?

3. How Can You Reduce The Load ....
   Or Make It Easier To Carry?

1

Do You Feel Like You're Carrying A Heavy Load ....

And Sometimes It's Just Too Much?

We all feel this way now and then. Sometimes we just feel like more demands are being made on us than we can handle. We can't avoid them all even if we want to, so we need to learn how to cope with them.

Stress is simply our response to the demands of daily living. We experience stress as we change and adapt to the events of our lives, pleasant or unpleasant, familiar or unfamiliar, lengthy or brief, simple or complex. We don't want to avoid stress completely. In fact, too little stress is as difficult to live with as too much, which is why solitary confinement is seen as a severe punishment. We all need activity, stimulation, challenge, and variety.

OVERLOAD: THE PROBLEM

But what if we feel that we have too much stress in our lives? This can definitely be a problem. Listen to the feelings people express when life's demands seem overwhelming:

> "My life feels hassled and rushed, like I have had my foot pressed against the accelerator."

> "It seems like there are not enough hours in the day to complete my work. Then when I do go to bed I can't fall asleep because I'm thinking about how much I have to do tomorrow."

> "I've had headaches and backaches and I've been prone to frequent colds and bronchitis. I'm also being treated by an endocrinologist for a hormone imbalance that is stress related. It's a

vicious cycle. I experience stress, react by overeating, gain weight, feel bad about myself (i.e. 'I'm fat and unattractive, no wonder no one ever asks me out on a date'), which contributes to the stress and the cycle repeats itself over and over."

"I'm trying to think about so many things and do so much that I can't stick to any one thing and finish it."

"I feel I have no control over my emotions — like they are independent of my actions. I feel panicky to a point of disorganization."

"My feelings of inadequacy and failure are almost unbearable. I feel isolated, like I am the only one who has these problems."

"I feel constantly dissatisfied with myself and afraid nothing will work out like I want it to. I see all the negatives ... I seem to lose interest in almost everything and can't find the motivation to pull myself out of this rut."

Sometimes we reach a point where all the worries, anxieties, and irritations add up to one big overload, or a major problem or demand comes along and uses so much energy that we don't have any left for other concerns, even small ones. Then we start feeling like it takes all the running we can do to stay in the same place!

BALANCE: THE KEY

What we are really looking for is **balance.** We each need to find the right level of stress to be happy, and then learn to live so that we can stay at that level. This is possible for all of us, but we have to work at it. Generally, we haven't been taught to recognize all the demands that add stress, the early signs of too much stress, or what to do when we realize we are overloaded. If we want to learn to manage our stress level more comfortably we will have to change our old habits. This is not terribly difficult but it will take work.

In this book we are going to teach you some simple ways of managing stress. We have taught these techniques to thousands of people in workshops and classes, and we use them ourselves in our own lives, so we know they are easy to learn. You can pick up these procedures quickly as you read the instructions and examples. Then, as you try them out, you can decide for yourself how they affect your experience of life. You can choose the methods you prefer, the ones that work best for you, and make them a regular part of your daily living. This will start you on the road to being a more relaxed, happier, and fulfilled person.

STRESSFUL SITUATIONS

What leads to that overburdened feeling? Let's look at a couple of examples:

> Norma has been feeling overloaded all winter, ever since she and her brother decided to put their mother in a nursing home. They both work, and they just couldn't take care of their mother after she had a stroke. But Norma feels guilty about putting her mother in the home. She visits her mother several times a week, which is hard because she has a full-time job, and a husband and two children at home who need her time and energy too. "I just feel like I'm running all the time," Norma says, "but I can't keep up and I'm always so tired."
>
> George feels like his life is over. Two months ago he got laid off from his job, and things don't look good for getting a job as good as the one he had because he is fifty-five. His wife has a job, but with the high cost of living it is hard to make it on her salary. The worst thing though is that George feels like a failure — out of work and not really knowing what to do. "I try to seem cheerful when people ask me how things are going," says George, "but really I just hate to get out of bed in the morning."

Both Norma and George are experiencing too much stress in their lives. To deal with what is going on, they are using a lot of physical and mental energy, and because of this they don't have much left for daily living. Probably they are also experiencing signs of distress such as headaches, backaches, upset stomach, frequent colds, or chronic tiredness.

YOUR REACTIONS

You may be saying, "Yes, but what can they do? Their situations are pretty hopeless." In one way you may be right. They may not be able to do much about the main events that they see as the causes of their stress. Norma will probably have to keep her mother in the nursing home, and George may not be able to find the kind of job he wants. There is something they **can** change, though. They can change the way they define the situation and what they decide to do to cope with it. Norma may have no good alternative to keeping her mother in the nursing home, but it is not necessary for her to feel guilty about it and run herself ragged trying to atone. George may have to settle for a job that is not his first choice, but he doesn't have to see himself as a failure and experience his life as empty and useless because of this.

What Norma and George **can** change, and what we can all change to get rid of that overloaded feeling, are our attitudes. The events in our lives do not **cause** us to feel overwhelmed; the stress is created by our attitudes toward these events. If specific situations were direct causes of stress, then everyone in these circumstances would feel equally stressed. You don't need to look very far to see that some people thrive in conditions that others find unbearable.

MORE STRESSFUL SITUATIONS

We'll talk more about this later when we get to specific techniques that are useful in changing the attitudes that lead to stress overload. Now, let's look at some examples of other ways of living that contribute to that overloaded feeling:

Mike

Mike prides himself on always doing a good job at what he sets out to do. Lately, though, he's been feeling like he just can't do enough. He's been working a lot of overtime and he's been hoping to get a promotion soon, so he wants to do an especially good job. He's heading up the fund raising committee for the new building for his church and this summer he's been coaching his son's Little League team. In their spare time, Mike and his wife have been remodeling their basement into a family room so the kids will have a place to entertain their friends. "It just seems like there aren't enough hours in the day," complains Mike. "Everything I'm doing is important to me, and I want to do a first-class job, but I don't know how I'm going to find the time."

Marcia

Marcia is a working mother who doesn't let her job interfere with taking care of her family. Sometimes, though, she feels like she's so rushed that she wonders if having the job is really worth it, even though they do need the money. Marcia does her grocery shopping in the evenings, sometimes going to several different stores to take advantage of specials. She always cooks good meals for her family, like her own mother used to make, and after dinner she spends time playing with the kids or helping them with their homework. On weekends she cleans the house, does the laundry, and tries to find time for at least one family outing. Also, Marcia and her husband occasionally go out or have friends over. "The problem is," says Marcia, "that everyone expects so much of me that I never have any time for myself. I wish I knew how other people manage."

BREAK THE TENSION SPIRAL

Both Mike and Marcia have themselves caught up in a tension spiral that could lead to trouble. Research shows that people under excess stress are more susceptible to illness, probably because stress lowers the body's defenses. Studies have connected stress to high blood pressure, heart disease, peptic ulcers, diabetes, ulcerative colitis, asthma, arthritis, multiple sclerosis, genital herpes and several forms of cancer. Investigators have also found that we are more likely to get everyday illnesses such as colds and flu during times of high stress.

It is possible to break the tension spiral, however, by changing your habits and learning to relax. If you begin to manage your stress, you can not only reduce your chances of getting sick, you can live a healthier, happier, and very likely a longer life. To do this, you will need to actively work at learning to change your lifestyle — just as Mike and Marcia will if they decide to change their way of living. Mike, for example, will need to decide which of his activities are the most important to him, and give priority to those while others wait for a while. Both he and Marcia need to set aside time for themselves every day to do something truly relaxing. To begin using stress management techniques, they may each have to give up something else. As compensation, they will feel much more alive and energetic.

Listen to some transformations people report after initiating some of the stress management techniques we teach:

> "I feel like I've been walking through the jungle for many years, and finally I've come to a clearing."
>
> "I now feel I can breathe without choking."
>
> "I am more relaxed about myself, my thoughts are less scattered, and I no longer fight my feelings. The flow of where I'm moving fits together in remarkable ways and life seems to become easier and more satisfying as it becomes more even."
>
> "I have learned that I have to do less in order to survive. The frustration I felt by not being able to maintain an excellent performance in every sphere of my life was clearly an unreasonable demand to place on myself. Letting myself off the hook was a tremendous relief!"
>
> "Always in the past, when I dealt with loneliness, anxieties and stress, alcohol was a nice companion to cover up pain. Lately, I've found I have no need or desire to drink. The inner peace and strength is constantly growing, and at times is amazing to me. It's like I'm on a natural high to life."

"I pay more attention to others. Being attuned to myself, both mentally and physically, has made me more sensitive to emotional needs of people in general. I have learned to listen, watch and communicate more effectively."

"I have come to realize that life can be whatever a person makes of it."

"I feel good about being me. I feel a sense of well-being and self-worth. I feel loving and loved. Is there any greater value? Not for me!"

Later in this book, we will provide you with specific instructions for techniques which will help you emerge from your "jungle" of stress. Before we begin that, it is important for each of you to take a long look at yourself, your attitudes and beliefs, and your habits, so you'll have a better understanding of where your overload is coming from and why you have trouble coping with stress.

2

What Is The Load...........

And Why Is It So Heavy?

Our lives are full of possible sources of distress — called stressors. Although extreme conditions such as floods or tornados are experienced as stressful by virtually everyone involved, most circumstances bring about more variable responses. Ordinarily, what is a stressor for one person may not be a stressor for another. People differ in the ways they interpret and react to specific events and in their sensitivity to situations. For example: some people love crowded, noisy parties, while others find such gatherings difficult and tiring; some thrive in jobs with continual interruptions, while others prefer working quietly alone.

ASSESSING YOUR STRESS LEVEL

Since you know yourself better than anyone else does, your own assessment of the stressors in your life and the amount of stress you are experiencing is very important. If you consider possible sources of stress in various areas of your life, you will be better able to develop an understanding of how much stress is comfortable for you and in what areas of your life you are experiencing too much or too little stress. After all, you wouldn't try to fix your car without first trying to find out which part or parts were causing the problem. The same approach makes sense for yourself.

You may have already taken either the brief or comprehensive version of the stress assessment we created, *Preventive Measures' Computerized Stress Inventory*. If so, you should have received your individual stress profile report, which discusses your stresses and strengths and recommends specific chapters in this book that will be most useful to you in improving your coping skills. If you would like to take our test, but can't find it available in your area, write to us at the address on the last page of this book and we'll send you information about how you can easily get it.

Perhaps you have evaluated your stress level using some other test. If so, consider the results carefully and try to determine which areas of your life seem to be your major sources of stress. Pay particular attention to any recommendations for change.

If you don't have any systematic evaluation of your stress levels available, we suggest that you take a hard look at four areas of your life — your work, your leisure time, your social life, and your close relationships — to begin to identify your stressors. To facilitate this process, we have included some questions that will help you judge for yourself, for each area, whether the level of stress is in balance or causing problems.

Answering these questions will not give you a formal "stress score." Thinking carefully about these issues **will** give you insight into what bothers you and how effectively you are dealing with particular problems in your life. (If you also want a more formal evaluation, contact us or go to a local wellness center, counseling center, psychologist or physician.)

INSTRUCTIONS FOR SELF-ASSESSMENT

To answer the questions, you will need four pieces of paper. Label them WORK, LEISURE TIME, SOCIAL LIFE, and CLOSE RELATIONSHIPS, respectively. Now, for each area, write down brief answers to the questions given below. Answer as honestly as you can — remember it is **yourself** you are trying to help.

Work

1. **How do you feel on the way to work in the morning?**
   __Do you feel tense and rushed?
   __Do you feel worried?
   __Are you alert?
   __Are you looking forward to the day?

2. **What do you do at work during breaks?**
   __Do you continue to think about work?
   __Are you bored?
   __Are you tense?
   __Are you relaxed?
   __Are you more refreshed after the break than before?

3. **How do you feel when working against a tight deadline?**
   __Do you feel confused?
   __Are you tense?
   __Do you feel confident you will finish?

4. **How do you feel during an interview with superiors?**
   __Do you feel scared and nervous?
   __Do you talk too much or too little?
   __Are you relaxed?
   __Are you able to present yourself well?

5. **How do you deal with demands from several sources at once?**
   __Do you feel overwhelmed?
   __Are you tense?
   __Do you look for an escape from the situation?
   __Can you set priorities calmly?

6. **How do you feel about your work in general?**
   __Do you feel like you can never catch up?
   __Are you bored with your job?
   __Do you feel that your job is challenging?
   __Do you feel you are capable of meeting the challenges?

7. **In summary, now that you have answered these questions about work, how would you describe the overall level of stress in that area of your life?**
   __Do you feel too little challenge in your work — are you bored?
   __Do you feel too much pressure in your work — are you hassled and overwhelmed?
   __Do you feel a balanced level of demand in your work — is it stimulating, interesting and energizing?

Leisure Time

1. **How do you feel when you have time off from work?**
   __Do you feel worried and guilty about the work you "should" be doing?
   __Do you rush around trying to make every minute fun?
   __Are you always busy taking care of your house, yard, etc.?
   __Do you feel relaxed?
   __Are you enjoying yourself?

2. **How do you feel when you are playing sports and games?**
   __Do you feel tense and worried about how you will perform?
   __Do you get tired easily?
   __Do you get bored easily?
   __Do you feel relaxed and confident?

3. **How do you feel when you are planning a vacation?**
   __Do you feel worried about spending too much money?
   __Do you worry about all the things that could go wrong?
   __Are you afraid of flying?
   __Do you worry about whether your companions (or family) will have a good time?
   __Are you relaxed and looking forward to the trip?

4. **How do you feel when working on a hobby?**
   __Do you find it hard to unwind enough to enjoy it?
   __Do you have a hard time finishing projects?
   __Do you get bored easily?
   __Are you relaxed and interested?

5. **How do you feel when trying to go to sleep?**
   __Do you have trouble relaxing?
   __Do you toss and turn?
   __Do you worry about events of the day or tomorrow?
   __Can you relax and go to sleep easily?

6. **In summary, now that you have answered these questions about your leisure time, how would you describe the overall level of stress in that area of your life?**
   __Do you feel too little enthusiasm in your leisure time — are you bored?
   __Do you feel too much tension to really enjoy your leisure time — are you rushed and worried?
   __Do you feel a balanced level of involvement in your leisure time — is it exciting, relaxing and fun?

Social Life

1. **How do you feel when you are introducing yourself socially?**
   __Are you nervous and uncomfortable?
   __Are you worried about how people will see you?
   __Do you feel comfortable?
   __Do you feel confident?

2. **How do you feel when you are talking to strangers at a party?**
   __Are you worried about what to say next?
   __Do you feel that they probably aren't interested in you?
   __Do you get bored easily?
   __Are you relaxed?
   __Are you enjoying yourself?

3. **How do you feel when you express an unpopular opinion in a social gathering?**
   __Do you feel anxious and embarrassed?
   __Do you feel confused and try to change the subject?
   __Do you get angry and defensive?
   __Do you feel comfortable with the fact that others don't agree with your views?

4. **How do you feel when you entertain others in your home?**
   __Are you worried that things won't go well?
   __Do you feel that everything has to be perfect?
   __Do you feel easily bored and ready for guests to leave?
   __Are you relaxed and enjoying yourself?

5. **How do you feel when you get bad service in a restaurant or hotel?**
   __Are you frustrated and anxious because you don't feel comfortable when making a complaint?
   __Do you feel that "this is just the way things are these days"?
   __Do you feel comfortable asserting your rights?

6. **How do you feel when listening to others talk?**
   __Do you feel anxious about how to respond?
   __Do you think of lots of terrific comments to make, but don't get the chance to say much?
   __Are you bored with much of the conversation?
   __Do you listen to others?
   __Are you interested in what others have to say?

7. **In summary, now that you have answered these questions about your social life, how would you describe the overall level of stress in that area of your life?**
   __Do you feel too little involvement in your social life — are you bored?
   __Do you feel too much strain in your social life — are you worried and anxious?
   __Do you feel a balanced level of participation in your social life — are you comfortable and confident?

Close Relationships

1. **How do you feel about inviting close friends to spend time with you, or about asking for a date?**
   __Are you worried about being rejected?
   __Do you think about asking, but just can't bring yourself to do it?
   __Do you feel relaxed and confident?

2. **How would you describe your relationship with your wife/ husband/partner?**
   __Are things tense between you?
   __Do you have many unresolved arguments?
   __Do you resent each other, or feel you are being taken advantage of?
   __Is your relationship joyful?
   __Is your relationship rewarding for both of you?

3. **How do you react when someone in your family does some thing that displeases you?**
   __Do you lose your temper quickly?
   __Do you get confused and upset?
   __Can you tell them calmly how you feel?

4. **How do you feel about your sexual relationships?**
   __Do you often feel anxious or worried about how you will perform?
   __Do you worry about feeling rejected?
   __Are you often bored?
   __Are you unresponsive during sex?
   __Do you enjoy sexual experiences?
   __Do you find that you are totally involved?

5. **How do you feel when a close friend or partner makes an unwelcome request?**
   __Do you agree even though you don't want to?
   __Do you feel tense?
   __Do you try to think of excuses to refuse?
   __Can you say no without feeling guilty?

6. **In summary, now that you have answered these questions about your close relationships, how would you describe the overall level of stress in that area of your life?**
   __Do you feel too little involvement in your close relationships — are you bored?
   __Do you feel too much tension in your close relationships — are you angry, resentful, or guilty?
   __Do you feel a balanced level of intimacy in your close relationships — are they joyful and rewarding?

AWARENESS OF STRESS

The questions you have just answered should help you become more aware of the habits, values, beliefs, situations and actions that contribute to stress in your life. They will also provide you with a picture of how you cope and how much control you feel over your own reactions.

To give yourself a clearer picture of your stress patterns, make a chart like the one below and fill it out for each of the four areas of your life you just examined. This is not a scientific measuring instrument; it is simply a way to look at your own stress patterns.

In each of the four areas, look at how you responded to the last question. Then make a mark on each life-area line to indicate the way you are feeling in that part of your life. Now, connect the marks to see your pattern. This will indicate which of the four areas of your life feel balanced to you and which feel stressful. You will probably want to remember your responses to this section as you read through the rest of this book.

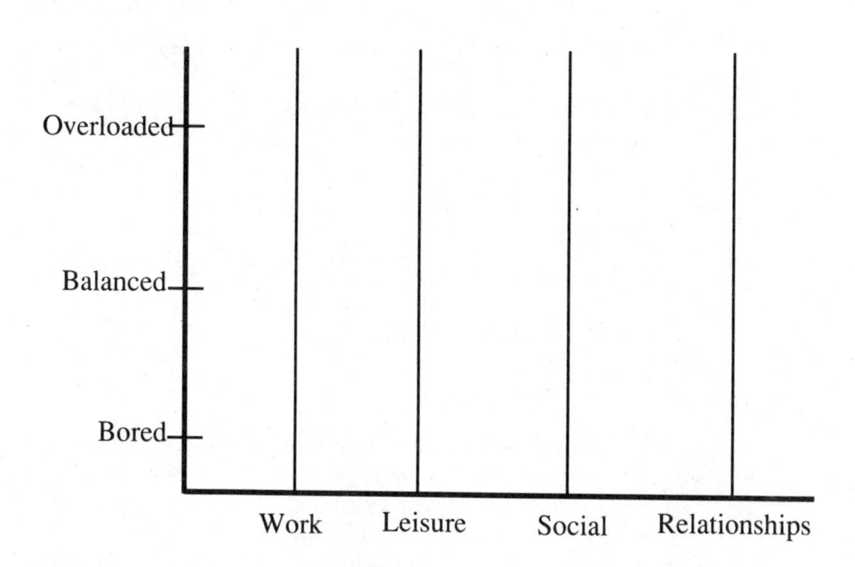

HOW YOU EXPERIENCE STRESS

Knowing how you physically experience stress is also important. If you are aware of where in your body you are most likely to feel tension, you may be able to do something about it when your body is just beginning to react, rather than waiting until you feel overwhelmed or incapacitated.

Look at the chart you just filled out. For each of the areas where you feel overloaded or bored, think about how this stress affects you physically and make a list of your physical symptoms. For example, do you get headaches? Backaches? Upset stomach? A tight face and clenched jaw? Keep these physical symptoms in mind as you read the rest of this book.

WHY YOU NEED TO KNOW YOURSELF

It's easy to feel stuck and frustrated when you're feeling a lot of stress in your life. You keep hoping your life will change for the better, but somehow it just stays the same or gets worse. One common reason for this is that most people aren't aware of the choices they have available for change. As we grow up we learn certain ways of dealing with life's difficulties. These methods may work for the original problems, but when we try to generalize the coping strategies to other situations we often find them ineffective. But, if we don't have any good substitute approaches, we may continually go back to the old ineffective ones — which is why we feel stuck.

Often it is the physical symptoms of stress overload that we notice first — although it may take a while before we actually accept these complaints as connected to our own lifestyle choices. The following account by a young woman in one of our classes illustrates the way stress-related complaints can grow to dominate your life.

Debbie: Tension Headaches

> I had not had a real problem with stress until the last couple of years. I had begun to experience some symptoms of stress in college around the time of finals. I had a rather funny experience, which wasn't funny at the time, but now I can look back on it and laugh and be a little embarrassed. ...
>
> I began to experience severe headaches that would last for several hours with some slight back pain. These began around Thanksgiving my senior year in college. I became concerned because I had never had headaches in my life. I went to my family doctor thinking the worst. My doctor talked to me a little bit about headaches and neckaches being related to overwork and worry and strain. I thought about that and made an effort to ignore these headaches but they continued. My doctor said he could do an X-ray but he really didn't think it was necessary. I decided to go ahead and have the X-ray. It of course showed nothing, which put my mind at ease somewhat. ...
>
> After this I finally realized that these headaches were, as the doctor said, a result of tension and stress. Boy did I feel dumb! I

had thought I was too young to be affected by stress. It was a foreign word, something that only high-powered executives with triple-bypasses suffered from. So, at the Christmas break, things calmed down, finals were over, and I didn't have any more headaches. I forgot all about it then and didn't let it worry me or bother to do anything about it. ...

The next time headaches bothered me was about two years later. I was out of school and had begun working. I moved into my own apartment and was finally on my own. By this time stress had been on the news a little bit and it was a subject that I was more aware of and knew a bit more about. I knew then that there were things you could do to lessen some of the stress and make it much easier to live with. However my headaches were only occasional and I really didn't worry about it much. ...

When I got married about a year later and moved to the city, I found a job after much searching. This is when I began to experience serious problems with stress and realized that I was responsible for dealing with this problem and it was something I had better face. ...

I was unemployed for about two months before finding a job in the city. My husband is a salesman who is gone Tuesday through Friday. I was new in town and didn't know anyone. My husband was just beginning in sales, working strictly for commission. I was so relieved to get a job that I thought things would settle down. However this job had an incredible amount of built-in stress that I had never believed possible.

My supervisor had told me that the position really required two full-time people and that I would be lucky to keep above water. It got to the point where I had a headache and neckache daily by noon. I would break out in a cold sweat or perspire for no reason at any given time. All weekend I would dread Monday and think about work and the people at work instead of relaxing and distancing myself from the situation. I would have a hard time getting to sleep on weekend or weekday nights. ...

On Sunday nights I would munch on something constantly. I could eat a whole bag of cookies (my favorite junk food) easily and eat more. It almost seemed better for me if I did not have a weekend break; it seemed easier if I knew I was going back to work tomorrow. I at times would experience rapid heartbeats for seconds or minutes at a time. Some days when I had been on the go more than usual, I would even become dizzy standing up; after a short time this would pass. I assumed it was just fatigue. I was always tired and felt pretty gray most of the time.

DECIDING TO CHANGE

At this point Debbie finally decided that her situation was unacceptable and that she must make some changes in her life. While you may not be feeling as uncomfortable as Debbie was, if you're like most of us, you'd like to change a few things in at least one area of your life, and you probably have a good idea of where the changes would be most welcome.

Now, of course, you want to know just how to go about making these changes — and that's what we are going to talk about in the next sections of this book. You'll also hear more from Debbie and from other people who have decided to take charge of managing their own stress levels.

3

How Can You Reduce The Load...........

Or Make It Easier To Carry?

Most of us occasionally find ourselves feeling overloaded and overwhelmed by stress. When that happens, we may react in one of several ways. Let's look at a few examples.

Don: Stress-related Illness

Ever since the company where he works was reorganized by the new management, Don has been feeling a lot of pressure and tension. Everything is confusing at work now. Nobody seems to know exactly what is going to happen or whether everybody will be kept on or not. Don has been getting a lot of stomach aches lately, and twice has had to be taken to the emergency room in the middle of the night because the pain was so bad. The doctors have done x-rays and tests, but so far haven't found any physical cause for the pains. "I think it's this damn job,", says Don. "It just makes me sick every time I think about it. I don't know what to do. I guess I'll just have to stick it out and see what happens."

Karen: Drugs As A Coping Method

Karen and her husband have been having a hard time getting along for about a year now. Karen feels like they just don't agree on anything anymore — on how to spend their money, how to bring up the kids, who to have for friends, or even what movies to go to. A few months ago, Karen asked her doctor to give her something to help her feel less tense because all the arguments were making her extremely upset and nervous. He prescribed a tranquilizer, and now Karen takes them every day. "I guess I shouldn't take them so often," says Karen, "but it sure makes things a lot easier to deal with. Maybe in a while we'll be getting along better and then I can stop taking them."

Vince: Alcohol To Reduce Stress

Vince has trouble talking to people. He never has found it easy to make friends and since he moved away from home to go to trade school he's been pretty lonely. He has found, though, that when he drinks it is easier to talk to people, and he feels that people like him more. He's found a few good bars where he feels comfortable, and he hangs out there in most of his spare time. A couple of weekends ago he got so drunk he doesn't even remember how he got home. "I sure have been getting some heavy hangovers lately," says Vince. "A couple of times I couldn't even get to school the next day. But pretty soon I'll have more friends here, and then I won't drink so much."

THE CHOICE: HEALTHY OR UNHEALTHY COPING

Don, Karen, and Vince provide us with some clues to why people experience problems in the way they deal with stress. We have already talked about the problem of illness resulting from stress. In a way, getting sick provides some relief from the stressful situation by temporarily removing ourselves from it. That is not to say people consciously plan it that way, but only that it sometimes works that way.

When people actually think about needing relief from stress, they often turn to drugs or alcohol. The strong appeal of drugs and alcohol as remedies for stress overload is that they **do** make you feel better — for a while. All you have to do is swallow something and you can forget all your cares, have a good time, and not let anything get to you. The **problem** is that these remedies do not actually solve anything, and they often have side effects. Furthermore, frequent reliance on these remedies can lead to even worse problems. Alcoholism and drug abuse are a major health problem in today's society.

Looking at the situations of Karen and Vince, it is obvious that they are not dealing with their problems directly; they are only trying to blot out the feelings they don't like. Their hopes that "pretty soon everything will be better" seem as unrealistic as their intentions to give up alcohol or drugs when their lives improve. It is unlikely that their lives will change positively until they decide to fundamentally alter their situations instead of just trying to get by.

Choice is the key here. Don, Karen and Vince have choices as to how they deal with their stressful predicaments, and we also have choices. People are not machines that have to blow a fuse every time our circuits are overloaded. We may not be able to transform the stressful situation, but we can change the way we react to it.

People are not accustomed to seeing the available choices because they are stuck in their traditional ways of looking at the world. When they are in a situation they don't like — one that they find stressful — they blame the situation, and if they can't change it, they react to it. Now they may be **right** that it is the situations that **should** change, but changing it may not be within their power. They **can** change the way they deal with the problem however, and that's where stress management training comes in.

It is not easy to change the way you deal with stress. If it **were** easy, everyone would already be doing it and no one would need books like this. The reason it isn't easy is that you have to break old habits and patterns, become more aware of your feelings and behavior, and take a long look at what your choices are.

It can be done, though, and **you** can do it, no matter who you are or what your past experience has been, if you meet one condition. That condition is that you must **decide** to put forth the energy to change your life. No one else can do it for you. We can teach you the techniques, and as we've said they are easy to learn. But **you** are the only one who can decide to use the techniques — and you have to **use** them to get the benefit.

TAKING CHARGE: DEBBIE SPEAKS AGAIN

Remember Debbie's description in the last chapter of the way stress was dominating her life? She had reached a dreadfully low point. But, as you will hear, she was able to make some remarkable changes when she finally decided to take charge of her own stress level.

> I began to realize that this situation was extreme and unacceptable. I decided I simply was not going to allow myself to continue this way. It was not only affecting me physically, with long-term effects I could only wonder and worry about, but it was affecting my whole perspective and my daily interactions with people. I made some personal goals about what to do about my career and how this would affect my personal life.
>
> I started with some small things on my job. I insisted on taking my half-hour lunch with no interruptions. The only unpaid overtime I put in was on required events. I refused to put in any more overtime. If the work was there today, it would be there tomorrow. I let people who put demands on me know that everything could not be top priority. I began to make people clearly state their dissatisfactions to clear the air of petty grievances, and began referring

some people to others better equipped to handle their problems.

These things were not easily done as I like to please others, especially employers. So, making the changes was to some extent stressful although they did give me some peace of mind.

However, as I looked at the way I had dealt with stress in the past and realized that I was going to be dealing with some stressful situations for the rest of my life, I decided I needed to investigate some practical solutions that would be effective for me.

At this point Debbie began to use specific techniques from this book to change her lifestyle. Again, it took some work, but she found the results worth the effort.

When I first began to read *Stress? Find Your Balance,* I could see right away the practical applications to my life. I read through the whole book the same day and reread parts to refresh my memory in deciding which parts to use.

I used all components of the book to some extent, but concentrated especially on exercise, nutrition and meditation. Embarking on this eight-week project was a scary prospect for me and not an easy thing for me to undertake.

A real motivating factor for me was the idea that I can have some control over my life, because I knew I really needed to get control. I felt physically bad a lot of the time and knew it would only get worse in the future. I could see a chance to try one or two things, really measure how they helped or didn't help, and then use that information for me.

Debbie started by changing her diet, which had consisted primarily of sugar. Although replacing sweets with healthier foods was a struggle, she was soon feeling so much better and more energetic that she felt encouraged to continue. She also started a regular walking program in the evenings after work, which she said left her feeling more cheerful and relaxed.

An unexpected bonus for Debbie was finding that in setting aside time for exercise, she had in a sense set aside time for herself. She used her walking time to rethink the day's problems, plan the next day, or just let her mind drift to pleasant thoughts. During the day she knew she had that time to look forward to and count on for herself.

The meditation exercises were difficult for Debbie at first. She sometimes felt dizzy or had trouble freeing her mind from outside concerns. She continued and now finds the meditation relaxing, although she still feels that she needs more time and practice to get the true benefits.

Debbie was especially interested in the ideas from the sections on looking at the world differently, giving up being right, dealing with criticism, putting yourself in someone else's shoes, and needing approval from others. She began to recognize how easily she fell into ways of thinking that caused her stress, and started using the suggested activities to help her stop and think about her choices of reactions.

At the end of her eight-week experiment, Debbie reported on her progress:

> I feel that I have succeeded because I intend to continue using all the things I learned. I dread even the thought of going back to feeling as badly as I used to. Now that I know I can choose to live my life feeling good, I plan to keep it that way.

MAKING HEALTHY CHOICES

In the remainder of this book we will give you specific instructions for the techniques Debbie used and for other procedures that have been found to be effective in managing stress. We'll also tell you how to set up a six- or eight-week plan to try some of them out the way Debbie did.

These methods have no undesirable physical side effects or aftereffects. They actually contribute to your good health. They do, however, require that you put forth the energy to incorporate them into your life — they are not instant cures!

We have organized the stress management techniques into two groups:

(1) Ways of making your load easier to carry.

These are routines that make you feel better in general, and allow you to deal with the irritations and crises of life in a calmer, more relaxed way.

(2) Ways of reducing your load.

These are processes that help you change the way you live so that you no longer experience so many events as irritating or stressful.

In each group we will provide you with a number of different procedures. You can try them all and then choose from each group the one or two which feel most comfortable and seem to best meet your needs. You will probably find that it works best to read only a chapter or two of this book each day, so you can try out the processes as you go.

After we have taught you the techniques, we will talk more about how you can incorporate them into your life as part of your regular routine. What you eventually decide to do to manage your stress overload will depend on your assessment of your stress levels and patterns, and on your experience as you practice the methods we provide.

We can't say that any one way of dealing with stress is the best way. We can only say that all of these techniques work, and that the best way for you to deal with stress is the way that works best for **you.**

SECTION 11 :

TECHNIQUES THAT MAKE YOU FEEL BETTER AND MAKE YOUR LOAD EASIER TO CARRY

4. RELAXING YOUR MUSCLES

5. MEDITATING

6. DOING MANTRA

7. EXERCISING REGULARLY

8. EATING RIGHT

9. EXPANDING YOUR AWARENESS

10. USING IMAGERY

4

Feel Better And Make Your Load Easier To Carry By...........

Relaxing Your Muscles

If you start noticing the way your body feels when you're tense, you'll discover that you store tension in certain parts of your body. Maybe you get a stiff neck, or tight shoulders, or maybe you get backaches. Or you may notice that your arms are tight, and you have made your hands into fists. Perhaps you clench your jaw and grit your teeth. Keeping your muscles tense like this leads to headaches, fatigue, and that overall tense, nervous feeling that can make you want to reach for tranquilizers or alcohol. There is another way you can get rid of this tension — and that is by consciously relaxing your muscles.

RELAX WITHOUT CHEMICALS

Relaxing your muscles by doing a deep-muscle relaxation exercise gives you tension relief similar to the relief a muscle-relaxant chemical such as Valium gives you — but without the pill! The way this works is that you prevent your muscles from being tense by relaxing them, either consciously or with a pill. Your muscles **can't** be both tense and relaxed at the same time. So if you can learn to relax your muscles, you can get rid of many of the uncomfortable symptoms of stress.

We are going to teach you two body relaxation exercises that are easy to learn, and that you can do yourself in twenty or thirty minutes. After you try these exercises you will be amazed at how relaxed your body feels. When you have practiced one or both of these exercises for a while, you will find that you begin to be much more aware of tension building up in your muscles, and that you can quickly and deeply relax your body in five or ten minutes.

The key to using these techniques is practice. Try one now and then do one once a day for a few weeks. By then, you will probably be able to quickly go through your body and relax your muscles, either when you feel tense or before a situation that might lead to tension. Of course, you will still want to use an entire relaxation exercise often, especially when you are tense after a long day or when you have trouble going to sleep.

To try these exercises, you can take several approaches. The best way is to have someone else read the instructions to you very slowly while you are doing the exercise. Or, you can slowly read the instructions into a tape recorder, and then play the tape for yourself while you do the exercise. Or, just read through the instructions to yourself a few times until you remember them, lie down, and **slowly** give yourself the directions as you go through the exercise.

INSTRUCTIONS FOR DEEP MUSCLE RELAXATION

In this exercise you will be tensing and relaxing your muscles. Be careful how tightly you tense any part of your body that has been badly hurt or is physically painful.

1. Lie down on your back on a blanket or mat placed on the floor. If this is not possible, sit comfortably in a chair. Close your eyes. Relax your body and let your breath come naturally. Place your hands by your sides. Insofar as possible, keep your body still. Do not move any part of your body except the part that you are tensing.

2. Tighten your left foot, then your left calf, knee, and thigh as tightly as you can. Lift your leg off the floor and continue tightening these muscles. Hold this for 10-20 seconds. In this, as in the following steps, the longer you hold and the tighter you clench your muscles the more effective this exercise will be. Let your left leg drop to the floor. Relax! Feel the waves of tension rising from your leg.

3. Repeat the instructions above with your right leg.

4. Tighten the muscles in your anal-genital area as hard as you can. Relax ..... Again, notice the rising waves of tension leaving your body.

5. Tighten the muscles in your stomach and try to press the small of your back into the floor. Relax .....

6. Take a deep breath and tighten your chest area. Relax .....

7. Tighten your fists, forearms, arms. Lift both arms slightly off the floor. Tighten them harder. Relax .....

8. Tighten the area around your shoulders and neck by trying to raise and lower your chin at the same time, but do this only **half tight!** Relax .....

9. Tighten the area around your mouth by pulling back the corners of your mouth. Relax .....

10. Tighten the area around your forehead by raising your eyebrows as high as possible. Relax .....

11. Take a deep breath and tighten all your facial muscles by contorting your face and scalp into the **ugliest** position possible while keeping the rest of your body relaxed. Lift your head off the floor slightly. Relax .....

12. Now, go through all the parts of your body in the **same order**, but with your "**mind**." Put your "mind" in your left foot, and relax and massage the area around your toes, arch, heel, etc., mentally. Move up to your ankle and calf. Repeat this sequence with your right foot. Take your time and move up your whole body this way. Pay particular attention to each hand, wrist, and arm. Go through your whole body until you've mentally relaxed each part all the way up to the top of your head.

13. Take a breath into the pit of your stomach ..... hold it for 5 to 10 seconds ..... open your mouth wide and let out your breath. When you let out your breath, force it out with a "whoosh"! Now take a breath into your upper chest ..... hold it for 5 to 10 seconds ..... open your mouth wide, and again let out your breath with a "whoosh." Take one more breath into your upper chest and repeat the last procedure. Now let your breath come naturally. You may find yourself sinking into the floor. Completely relax .....

14. Come back by taking a deep breath into your lungs. Move your arms and hands. Take several minutes to **slowly** bring yourself back. Now open your eyes.

MODIFY THE EXERCISE TO SUIT YOUR NEEDS

If you only have a few minutes and are feeling tense, you can do a briefer (and consequently less relaxing) version of this exercise. If you have more time, and want an even deeper feeling of relaxation, you can do the exercise more slowly, dealing with each muscle group in your body individually.

Some people report muscle spasms when doing deep muscle relaxation. Mild spasms are common and should be ignored unless you feel uncomfortable. If your muscles start cramping painfully, move the affected part of the body until the cramping stops while leaving the rest of your body as relaxed as possible.

You may become so relaxed during deep muscle relaxation that you fall asleep. This is fine if you are using the exercise to help you get to sleep. If you don't want to fall asleep during the exercise but find that you often do, you may want to change the time of day that you do this exercise.

BENEFITS OF PRACTICE

A little practice with deep muscle relaxation will help you become much more familiar with your body and the way it reacts to stress. Then when you feel tension in a particular part of your body, you can tense and relax that part several times in succession. You will find this very helpful in monitoring stress building in your body. For example, one of our clients reported:

> After I had practiced this technique for awhile I became more aware of those times of increased stress levels and my body's reaction to stress. I extracted bits and pieces of the deep muscle relaxation technique and applied them throughout the day. For example, I would do "mental massaging" to relax my shoulders and neck area when I became aware of these muscles tightening. It felt great to be able to notice when stress was affecting me and be able to do something about it.

INSTRUCTIONS FOR IMAGERY RELAXATION

In this exercise, you will be creating in your mind a totally relaxing setting for yourself, one that involves lying on warm sand, hearing the sound of the ocean, and letting the warm ocean water wash over you. If you have a strong negative association to the ocean, you may want to rewrite this exercise using another setting that is equally relaxing, such as lying on your back in a meadow with the warm sun comfortably shining on you while a gentle breeze blows over you.

1. Lie down on your back on a mat or blanket placed on the floor, or sit comfortably in a chair. Relax your body and let your breath come naturally. Place your hands by your sides.

2. Imagine that you are lying on a beach. You can **feel** the warm sand under you while the sun warms you from head to toe. You can **hear** the waves from the ocean as they wash up against the shore. You can **smell** the salt water and **feel** a few drops of the ocean from the spray of the waves. Do whatever you need to do to create this image for yourself in your 'mind's eye'.

3. Now imagine that this warm ocean water runs up onto the shore and over your feet. These waves totally penetrate your skin, bones and sinew of your toes, heels, bottoms and sides of your feet ..... then this warm salt water runs back into the ocean, carrying with it any tension, pain, or distress that you were feeling in that part of your body.

4. Now this warm ocean water runs up a little higher, covering both your feet and your ankles. These warm ocean waves totally penetrate your feet and ankles. And as these waves run back into the ocean, any tiredness, tension or stress that was present in your feet and ankles is carried away.

5. Now these waves run up even higher, as far as your knees. Again, these waves totally penetrate your skin, bones, and muscles from the bottoms of your feet to your knees ..... and as this warm ocean water runs back into the sea, the water takes with it any negative feelings, any tiredness or pain you might be experiencing there.

6. Now this warm ocean water runs up even higher, as far as your waist. It totally penetrates the lower half of your body ..... and as the salt water runs back into the sea, it carries with it any feelings of anxiety, tension or pain that you might be feeling there.

7. Now the waves run midway up to your chest, totally penetrating your body from the middle of your chest down to the bottoms of your feet ..... and as the salt water flows back into the sea, it takes any pain or distress you might be feeling.

8. Now this warm ocean water runs up to your shoulders, totally covering your arms and body from the neck down. Again, this healing liquid penetrates your body completely ..... and as it runs back into the sea, it carries with it any feelings of anxiety, stress, or discomfort you might be experiencing.

9. Now this warm ocean water covers your **entire** body. You have no difficulty breathing because this healing liquid quickly penetrates your face and scalp along with the rest of your body ..... and as this healing ocean water runs back into the sea, it takes with it any tension, pain or discomfort you might still be feeling.

10. Imagine the waves running up your body and covering it completely several times. Imagine the warm ocean water penetrating your entire body ..... and then falling back into the sea, taking with it all of your fatigue, stress, and tension.

11. If there is any part of your body that still feels tense or stressed, direct the warm ocean water there. The warm water penetrates that part of your body ..... and then falls back into the sea, taking with it all the stress and tension in that part of your body.

12. Now take a few minutes to enjoy the feeling of comfort and vitality coursing through your body. Let your breath come naturally and let yourself completely experience the way your body feels.

13. Come back gently by taking a deep breath into your lungs. Move your arms and hands. Take several minutes to **slowly** bring yourself back before opening your eyes.

PEOPLE USING DEEP MUSCLE RELAXATION

Deep muscle relaxation is an easy procedure to use in coping with many of the stresses of daily life. Here are some examples of people using the technique to help them with a variety of problems:

Jack: Work Overload

When my work starts piling up, my body just doesn't want to cooperate. It begins to ache and tense up, and I often get severe headaches. I have used the deep relaxation techniques since I went to the stress management workshop last year. It works best for me if I am alone and in a dimly lit room. When I am finished, my body is rested, and most of the time my headaches are gone or at least dimmed. Then I can get on with my work.

Rita: Getting to Sleep

I have used the deep relaxation exercises to overcome insomnia. I found that when I couldn't sleep it was primarily due to two things: one being concerns that occupied my mind, and the second being physical tenseness, which was probably connected to the problems that my mind was dwelling on. The technique of deep relaxation has a two-fold effect for me. First by drawing attention to each part of my body, I am able to release the previously unnoticed tension. Then, because the focus of my mind is on the tenseness of my body and the subsequent release of that tension, I am no longer thinking about my problems. This release from concern, coupled with the physical release from tension, almost always puts me right to sleep.

Sandy: Stiff Necks

I don't like to rely on drugs if I can help it, so when I learned the deep muscle relaxation technique last year, I decided to try using that instead of pills when I got a stiff neck. A few weeks later I felt the tightness and stiffness beginning at the base of my neck and in my shoulders. I taped the instructions for the relaxation exercise, listened to the tape, and practiced the relaxation every day. I loved doing the relaxation, and eventually I was able to practice it without the tape. I found that in relaxing it not only relieved my stiff neck and shoulders but also made my entire body feel peaceful.

Ellen: Nervousness and Worry

During the first week I did deep muscle relaxation I didn't note any great changes in the way I felt, but I wrote that I felt good about doing something for myself that would make me a healthier person. I hadn't given myself that much attention before and through the second week I could tell that I was getting in touch with myself more. I started thinking about how worthless I had felt in the past, especially with the breakup with my boyfriend. I realized that it was important to take care of me!

Doing this exercise allowed me to take time out for myself and to realize that inner peace was very vital for me to truly find happiness. Not only was this good for me but I think it also made me a more caring and understanding mother and friend. I started noticing that I got less harried at the end of the work day. I began to look forward to my relaxation method in the evening. Before I might have stayed up too late because I couldn't get relaxed enough to sleep or I might have taken a drink to calm myself. Now I could go to bed and fall asleep right away.

By the third week I realized that I wanted the effects of these exercises to stay with me as long as possible. One way I started doing this was to slow myself down. In the past it was like I was always in a hurry or running late, or at least I felt that way. But I knew I did not like feeling anxious. So I would tell myself to slow down and I would take some deep breaths. I was more aware of when I was feeling anxious than before. I told myself it was okay and that I did have to be afraid of being anxious or try to get rid of the feeling with a pill. I want to be in control of my emotions without drugs, and I found it became easier and easier to take care of things as they happened and not to needlessly worry about what might happen.

Taking this class and doing these exercises have been a lifesaver for me. I guess I still consider myself to be a little prone to nervousness but I realize that it's just a state of mind. I'm not doomed to being a worry wart. I am who I am and what my future holds for me depends on how I handle it.

5

Feel Better And Make Your Load Easier To Carry By...........

Meditating

You may think meditation is a strange, magical, or mysterious practice used only by Hindu Swamis in dark caves in India. Actually, there is nothing mysterious about meditation. It is an amazingly simple technique that is easy to learn and has great benefits in reducing tension. People in all walks of life are meditating these days — businessmen, housewives, students, politicians, and others — now that the amazing benefits are becoming better known. You can learn to meditate in about 30 minutes, and if you take the time to meditate for about 20 minutes every day you will soon begin to feel powerful differences in your life.

WHAT IS MEDITATION?

Meditation is simply a general word for a number of related practices which bring about a kind of free-floating state of mind differing from our ordinary rational state of being. When meditating, words become far less important than usual, and you sense that you are close to being in touch with your "true" or "real" self. You become more open to experiencing your inner states and more open to your environment and friends as well.

All systems of meditation share a common theme: when meditating, you focus our attention on something and the outside world gradually becomes more distant. **What** you focus on depends on the system of meditation you are using. The focus may be a phrase or mantra, an object, your breathing, chanting out loud, a thought or idea, or witnessing the flow of thoughts through your mind. Some systems of meditation insist that you keep your thoughts focused on the object of your meditation; if your mind wanders you must shift it immediately back to the object of meditation. Other systems are more permissive, allowing the meditator more freedom to experience thoughts that may come up and return to the object of mediation more gently.

We are going to teach you a permissive system of meditation. Our emphasis is on your creating an accepting attitude towards whatever thoughts and feelings arise within you while you are meditating. We encourage you to create an open mind and accept whatever you experience without judging yourself.

At this point, it will be most useful if you actually experience what it is like to meditate. After you read the instructions, you will need about 20 minutes and a quiet place where you won't be disturbed. If necessary, you might want to unplug the phone. Now, carefully read the directions below and then .... meditate!

INSTRUCTIONS FOR MEDITATION

1. Choose one type of meditation.

These instructions will teach you two different types of meditation. In the first, you sit still with your eyes closed and focus attention on your breathing while you "let go" of all the thoughts that occupy your mind. In the other, you focus on a mantra or phrase that you "hear" in your mind.

Both types of meditation are very effective. We suggest you try one for a few days and then try the other so you can see which type you like better. For today, read the instructions for both types and choose the type you will try today, rereading those instructions before you begin.

2. Find a comfortable place.

For both types of meditation you begin by choosing a comfortable place where you won't be interrupted. You can sit on a pillow on the floor, or in a chair in a comfortable position. If you're using a chair, use one that has a straight back, possibly one with a high back that will support your head and shoulders. Your spine, neck, and the back of your head should be in a straight line. If you're sitting on a pillow on the floor, you can meditate in a cross-legged position. You will probably want to loosen your clothing and remove your shoes for added comfort. Your hands can be folded in your lap or placed over your knees. Get comfortable.

3. Center yourself.

Move your body slowly to the left and right, forward and back, until it feels "centered" or balanced. Do the same with your head and neck. Inhale and exhale through your nose rather than your mouth throughout the period of time you are meditating. Now you are ready to follow the instructions for the type of meditation you choose (either the **breathing** or the **mantra** meditation). Now, try the one you choose for 20 minutes.

4a. Breathing meditation:

Close your eyes and focus on your breathing. Take a slow, deep breath, breathing through your nose; think to yourself the word "in" as you breathe in, and "out" as you breathe out. After this first deep breath, let your breathing happen on its own, becoming fast or slow, deep or shallow as it will. Just think to yourself "in" on the in breath, and "out" on the out breath. If either of these words seems harsh to you substitute another. If you choose, expand each word in your mind so that it extends throughout the breath.

Do this meditation in an easy, relaxed way. If your mind wanders from your breathing, refocus it on your next breath. It is important not to evaluate your thoughts or your ability to stay with your breath. As your mind wanders, or you notice a sensation somewhere in your body, experience this as completely as possible in an accepting way. Then, when you are ready, let your focus of attention return to your breathing. If at any time the words fade out and you are sensing your breath alone, that's fine. The words are there only to give your mind something to occupy it. When your meditation is over, sit quietly for a few minutes.

4b. Mantra Meditation:

First, it is necessary to select a mantra (a word or phrase to repeat). If you choose, you can pick a word or a short phrase of your own that has a pleasant sound to you. Words or phrases like *peace, amen, let it be*, or others with positive connotations are fine. Avoid any words or phrases that have a negative emotional component. The word or phrase should feel harmonious and soothing as you say it to yourself. Alternatively, here is a Sanskrit phrase that makes an excellent mantra: *Om (Aum).*

Close your eyes and say the mantra to yourself slowly and rhythmically. As you repeat it to yourself, let it gradually go deeper and deeper inside you. Now, keeping your eyes closed, stop saying the mantra. Simply listen to the mantra in your mind. Do not say the word; rather, "hear" the mantra. In this meditation, then, you sit quietly, hearing the mantra. The mantra may occur in rhythm with your breathing, or it may not. Allow the mantra to change in any way it chooses — slower, faster, softer, louder, or disappearing and then returning. If you get caught up in your thoughts, fine. Experience these in a completely accepting way, and when you are ready return to your mantra. When your meditation is over, sit quietly for a few minutes.

QUESTIONS ABOUT MEDITATION

Now that you have tried meditating, you will probably have questions. Here are answers to some commonly asked questions:

Q: Can I meditate lying down?
A: It is best not to, since you are likely to fall asleep.

Q: When is the best time to meditate?
A: It is preferable to meditate twice a day for 10 to 20 minutes each time. Once a day for 20 minutes is also ok. If you meditate less than once a day, or for less than a total of 20 minutes you may not experience the benefits that people report who meditate for at least 20 minutes.

Q: What are these benefits I can expect to get from meditating?
A: Meditation brings about a general quieting of your body and mind. You enter a state of deep relaxation that resembles sleep or presleep. Your body uses less oxygen and your brain waves take on an overall harmonious or rhythmic quality. You experience your thoughts and feelings without evaluating them. If you meditate every day, you will find that you are more accepting of yourself and more able to focus completely on your activities of the moment. You will also find that fewer events seem stressful and that you deal with those that do in a calmer, more relaxed way. When you do feel tense, you will return to a relaxed state more easily.

Q: When I was meditating, I felt very light—like I was going to float away. This feeling scares me. What should I do?
A: When you begin meditating you may notice some strange or unpleasant sensations such as feeling very heavy or very light, or itching, tingling, or trembling. You also may hear music or other sounds, or see colors or images. You may suddenly feel angry or sad. Although these are common experiences, you will probably not notice more than one or two of them. They should have no aftereffects in your daily life. If such feelings disturb you, simply meditate less often or for a shorter time until the effects disappear. Then gradually increase your meditating to an optimal length.

Q: I can't keep my mind quiet. Thoughts keep distracting me while I meditate. What can I do?
A: First, accept the fact that thoughts will come up. The more you

meditate the more you come to realize that you are not controlled by your thoughts. You can choose to look at your thoughts, experience them, consider them, and then decide to shift the focus of your attention to your breathing or your mantra.

Q: You said at the beginning of this chapter that we shouldn't judge ourselves harshly because we have thoughts while we meditate. I still get upset with myself when I get distracted during my meditation and I judge myself even more when I notice myself getting upset. How can I stop this?

A: You are likely to evaluate yourself on how well you mediate even if you tell yourself not to. The best approach is to notice when you do this and gently decrease or stop it. One of our students reported:

> My mind has been wandering **a lot** during the entire two months I've been meditating. In the beginning I was very critical of myself for not being able to control this better. After a class discussion about this issue I decided to quit being so judgmental. I then began to focus on my breathing and just watch where my mind went when it wandered. Whenever I realized I was not paying attention to my breathing, I would just focus on it again. While it was difficult at first not to be critical of myself, with time it became easier.

Q: Sometimes I get bored when I meditate — terribly bored. Is this normal?

A: Boredom is a way people feel sometimes, as is happiness, sadness or any other emotional state. If you feel bored while meditating let yourself experience the boredom without judging or evaluating yourself. If you keep meditating the boredom will sooner or later disappear.

Q: Can meditating ever be bad for you?

A: A few people find meditating upsetting. They start experiencing emotions they can't handle. If this happens, it is best to either decrease the amount of time you are meditating or stop meditating altogether for a while.

Q: Is it ever advisable to meditate for more than two 20-minute periods a day?

A: In general it is not a good idea to meditate more than 40 minutes a day unless your meditations are being supervised. Prolonged meditation can result in being overwhelmed by difficult emotions. Occasional circumstances that may be exceptions include brief extremely stressful times or periods of forced inactivity. In times of unusual stress, you may not feel as calm as usual after your meditation, and may need to either extend your meditation an additional 20 minutes or meditate again after a short break. At times when you are required to rest because of injury or illness, you may want to meditate periodically throughout the day as a way of coping with the inaction.

Q: I seem to get into a deeper, calmer state when I meditate with another person or a group of people than when I meditate alone. Am I imagining this?

A: While we do not have an explanation for this phenomenon, many people report that meditating in a group is more satisfying than meditating alone.

PEOPLE USING MEDITATION

Judy: Accepting Herself

One of the primary benefits I get from doing mantra meditation is a feeling of "wholeness". While it took awhile, I've found that an important component is allowing myself to simply "be." I didn't recognize this at first. I thought I had to be achieving something like total relaxation and if I wasn't able to completely block out all thoughts except the mantra then I wouldn't be successful. In other words, it is important to be self-accepting. I have found it helpful to think of the meditation as a way of working toward creating twenty minutes of self-acceptance each day. When I am able to feel accepting of all my thoughts and feelings I come away from the experience with greater self-esteem.

Ed: Better Than Drugs

When I was an adolescent, drugs were an important part of my peer group, as well as something very cool and intriguing. I became quite involved, and only associated myself with people who "also knew where things were at." In retrospect, drugs were a way to experience my body, mind, music, and people in a new and exciting way. There were drugs to enhance every type of sensation and mood that I wanted. I took pride in knowing everything there was to know about them. I was fascinated with experiencing new things and the sky was the limit.

I was desperately looking for the ultimate experience, the high of highs. I was very lucky that I wasn't hurt during those years, yet somehow came through it all a lot wiser. For various reasons I got to a point where I felt I was becoming much too involved in the drug scene and wanted to get away from it. I therefore volunteered for the draft and began my military career. It wasn't long before I was on my way to Vietnam (and I thought I was getting away from drugs!). ...

Well I physically survived my year in Vietnam and came home. What nobody ever told me was how to deal with the aftermath. It isn't easy to start your life where you left off and pretend that the whole thing never happened. I no longer felt like I belonged anywhere. My personal relationships were being affected by my behavior. I was no longer the same person that I used to be.

One evening I met a guy who seemed to have an unusual calmness about him, an aspect I found unfamiliar. He told me about a meditation class he was attending and how meaningful it had been in his life. For some reason I checked it out. To make a long story short, I became involved and participated for approximately two years. ...

Meditation has become an essential part of my life. Prior to being involved with this class I surrounded myself with people who were also quite dissatisfied with society and angry. Smoking dope had become a way of life for us all. But after becoming seriously involved with meditation, I gave up getting high and being angry. Life has become more mellow and complete — my day-to-day life no longer seethes with meaningless tasks and boredom.

For me, meditation serves as a means of detachment and calmness. Things that previously would have provoked me to an angry response are now perceived as simply statements and not attacks on me personally. It has taken a long time, but I realize now that working on myself is the only way I can effect any type of change.

Linda: Coping With Office Conflict

When I first started to meditate I didn't know what to expect, as I had never done this type of thing before. I found that it was hard to let go of my thoughts since I was not used to sitting quietly for a period of twenty minutes. After I managed to get into the meditation, I found that my conception of time had very little to do with the reality of the situation. I would start the meditation at a certain time and continue with the breathing, relaxing and letting go. But usually my meditation lasted only ten minutes or so. Later, as I got more used to the technique, I became better at gauging the time; in other words I was better able to meditate for the full twenty minutes.

Because of some reading I had done on meditation, I think I expected instant results: that the benefits of using this technique would change my perspective on so many things; that peace, calm and tranquillity would be there for the taking. What I really found was that the art of meditation is not something that you pick up in a matter of a couple of attempts, but rather is a developed technique that is acquired after much practice. Since I am one of those people that is used to immediate results, it was frustrating for me to have to master something like this over a period of time. What I did not expect was what the benefits of meditation actually meant to me in the long run. ...

I was having a terrible time with my supervisor at work. I was not only upset about it, but was actually wondering if I could stand to work for this person any longer. It was not that I have never been through office politics, it was the type of situation. My supervisor's attitude towards another staff member was so biased that it was very hard for the other staff to get their jobs done. I have a real problem when I see people treated unfairly. I was supposed to accept the situation and like it, and I didn't.

This problem initially had a negative effect on my meditation, since I had a hard time concentrating on any other thing than the turmoil I was going through. This was such a low point in my life that I was wondering whether I could continue working in this kind of setting. When I did my meditation, I tried to let go of the negative feelings that I was having in regard to this man. I am not saying that I went into my meditation with only that intent, but it was something that I consciously thought about. ...

What I found in my meditation was the calmness that helped me get through this trying time. I did not resolve the situation, I accepted. I learned that I could accept things and not have to change them. I have spent so much time trying to find the answers to: Why? Why? and Why?

Asking "why" has had the effect of making me look at things too closely and trying to change things that really are not critical to me. I have learned from doing my meditation to let go and let go and to let go more and more. When I let go of the anger that I, myself, had created by focusing on this situation, I discovered that I, myself, was creating part of my supervisor's and my bad working relationship.

Today, I can look at this situation a little more clearly and objectively. I really do not have to hang on to the negative aspect of a person, but can look past that at some very positive things about that same person and, perhaps, focus on these things instead. I can respect him and myself for who we are and not for what we do. I feel that this has had such a positive effect on me that if this was all I had gained from this technique, it would be enough. ...

When I sit here thinking about how meditation has affected me, I also have to look at a change in my attitude. I am not nearly so hard on myself, because I can let go of that part that keeps telling me that I have to be perfect. I am not perfect, and I can accept that. I can accept what I can do and whatever small effect that I might have. It seems like I have had such an inflated picture of myself as the super person. When I could accept that I was only me, it made it so much easier to do whatever I had to do. ...

I lead a very hectic life. I am married and have a husband and three children to think of and care for. Even though my oldest children are fairly capable of looking out for themselves, they still demand time and attention. I have a full time job that takes up a lot of time and consideration, as well as a lot of thought. There are so many things that take my mind and time that sometimes it is very difficult not to become distracted.

Through meditation, I have found a way to devote some time to myself in a very quiet and calming way. It is very hard for me to find the time, much less take the time, to do some things for myself. So, when I decided to meditate, it meant that I would have to make a concerted effort and commitment to do this. If I had known of the benefits, I'm sure I would have tried it sooner.

I have found, through doing meditation, a calmness that I have been able to incorporate into many areas of my life. I believe that I am better able to get all of the things done that I have to get done, because of the twenty minutes I try to spend on meditation daily. This time is an important part of my life, and I intend to continue with it.

Will meditation work as well for you as it did for Linda, Ed and Judy? The only way you can find out is to try it for yourself and see.

6

Feel Better And Make Your Load Easier To Carry By...........

Doing Mantra

Sometimes your own thoughts create a stress overload for you. For example, you may be unable to stop thinking about something that you are angry or worried about. You may keep going over and over in your mind something upsetting that has happened, or that you think will happen. Or you may find yourself constantly judging your own behavior. Your conscience or "inner critic" constantly provides you with a list of "shoulds" and "musts", tormenting you when you do not follow them to the "inner critic's" satisfaction.

MANTRA CAN QUIET YOUR MIND

The use of **mantra** is one way of breaking the hold your thoughts have on you. This is easy to understand if you compare your mind to a lake. On the bottom of the lake is an object you are trying to see. You look down at the bottom but you can't see the object because the surface of the lake is covered with waves going in all directions, blocking your view. These waves coming from all directions are like your thoughts; with your thoughts coming from all directions your mind is never still or at peace.

Now, imagine that an artificial wave — not choppy like the other waves, but very regular — appears on this lake. All the other waves are taken over by this one wave. Soon, the lake becomes transparent again. Or, imagine oil is being poured on the lake. This "constant wave" or "pouring oil on water" can be produced in your mind simply by adding a new thought which is being regularly produced. When you do this, your mind starts to quiet as all other thoughts are taken over by one controlling thought. This thought then becomes a **mantra,** and saying this thought over and over again in your mind becomes the process of **doing mantra.**

HOW DO YOU DO MANTRA?

To do mantra you repeat inside your head one word or phrase over and over again. For example, if your mantra is the word *peace*, you silently say to yourself *peace, peace, peace, peace.....* You may find yourself saying this word faster or slower at times. Sometimes, it may be in tune with your breathing, at other times not. All of this is fine. Whenever your mind stops saying the mantra and you want to continue, simply start saying the mantra again without evaluating yourself for letting your mind wander. In doing this practice, you are **actively** saying the mantra to yourself. This is different from mantra meditation, and you should not use a mantra you use in meditating.

WHEN IS A GOOD TIME TO DO MANTRA?

Anytime you are by yourself, whether washing dishes, driving a car, cleaning, walking, etc., or in a situation where you are bored, angry, worried, or frightened by something that is happening or that you think might happen. In these situations and others, doing mantra can help you focus your attention, break old habits so that you are more open to the immediate experience around you, and help keep your mind from focusing on the past or anticipating the future.

Mantra can be used both in times of distress and as a general practice. When used in times of distress, it exerts a calming effect. When used as a general practice, all events start to be experienced as less stressful and more "ok" than they were.

It is a good idea, however, not to use the same mantra for both a general mantra and for times when you are experiencing extreme distress. If you use your general mantra in emergencies, the mantra becomes associated with the stress you are feeling at that time. Using the mantra when you are again feeling calm may evoke some of the stress you were previously experiencing. Using a different or "emergency" mantra in very stressful situations prevents this from happening.

Mantra is a **very powerful** device and it is important not to underestimate its value. It seems to bring benefits whether it is done regularly for fifty minutes a day or off-and-on for one to five minute periods during the day.

WHAT WORDS MAKE GOOD MANTRAS?

Almost any single word or short phrase that has a positive meaning for you makes a suitable mantra. Words or phrases such as:

PEACE
LET IT BE
I AM CONFIDENT AND CALM
I AM FILLED WITH JOY AND HAPPINESS
*OM or AUM (*the Sanskrit universal sound)
OM MANE PADME HUM (general Sanskrit mantra)

all make good mantras. Many religious phrases make good mantras. A good mantra becomes melodious and comfortable with use.

If using a particular mantra creates a feeling of discomfort, you should substitute another mantra. It is also essential that the mantra **not** contain a negative message for you. When you say a phrase over and over again, the meaning the phrase has for you literally becomes a part of you. If you frequently tell yourself things like, *I just can't win, Nobody cares*, or *Life is lousy*, you will experience life in those ways to any even greater degree than you did before.

Mantra can also be combined with imagery. For example, the mantra: *The power of God is within me, The grace of God surrounds me;* can be done in the following way:

> While saying the first sentence to yourself imagine a steel rod in the place of your spine. Experience the rod as unbreakable and the source of infinite power. Similarly, when saying the second sentence, imagine being surrounded by an unbreakable invisible shield. Other, similar images can of course be substituted.

Combining imagery with mantra, as in this example, can start a change in your self-image, a change in the direction of increased inner power and a greater feeling of safety and support.

WHAT ARE THE BENEFITS OF MANTRA?

Mantra quiets your mind when you are tense and worried and can't stop thinking about a problem. It helps your mind remain steady by giving it something to hold on to, namely the word or phrase you are repeating. Mantra can also help you defeat depression so that your life seems more even, and the joy in your life is easier for you to see.

USING MANTRA IN EMOTIONAL EMERGENCIES

A good example of using mantra to get through a difficult time is the story of Jill, who has just been told by Stan, her fiance, that he is breaking their engagement of the past four months. Jill, of course, found this devastating. She loved Stan very much and couldn't imagine life without him.

Jill also knew about mantra as a stress management technique. Since she was clearly experiencing extreme distress in the form of crying, depression, and symptoms of anxiety, she decided to choose a different mantra than the one she normally uses — a mantra she can use for emergencies like the present situation. She decided to try the mantra, *This too will pass* as a way of reminding herself that no matter how bad the situation, it will get better.

Over the next week Jill said this mantra whenever it occurred to her. While she didn't feel like her usual self, she noticed that she was crying less often, and not feeling as depressed or anxious as she thought she would be. By the end of the week it was really clear to her that while she missed Stan and wished he would change his mind and come back, she knew that she was still attractive and that she could have other relationships.

She decided to use the extra time she now had to see friends and acquaintances on a more personal basis than was possible when she was a part of a "couple." By the end of two weeks she was definitely close to normal, and in touch with the positive aspects of this breakup as well as the negative ones. She felt that if Stan did change his mind, she would be a stronger person by having experienced her ability to survive and take care of herself in a very difficult situation. In fact, she found that she was thinking better of herself than she had before this happened.

USING MANTRA IN DAILY LIFE

Lois: Help with family problems.

I knew absolutely nothing about doing mantra (and had never even heard of it) until it was discussed in class and I read about it in the book. I started using it and found that it works!

I have been having a lot of problems with my two teenagers that I just couldn't stop thinking about. When I find myself getting all worked up and stressed out, I begin repeating the phrase *let it be* over and over in my mind and sometimes out loud. It's wonderful because I begin to feel calm and am able to stop thinking obsessively about what is bothering me.

I use mantra several times a day now, at home, in my car, and at work. It is especially useful on the way home when I'm thinking about how I'm going to react to my kids. Usually if I do mantra, I can walk into the house and greet them calmly.

Rebecca: Less upset over little things.

I had always thought that to do mantra you had to use some strange foreign phrase or say OM-M-M-M out loud or something. However, to learn that I can repeat something as simple as *let it be* to myself over and over whenever I wanted to sounded worth trying, so I did.

The change I have noticed since using mantra is that I get less upset over little things, especially in interactions with people close to me. I am usually acutely aware of what is going on around me. I am often suspicious and anxious if I am not included in something.

Now when I find myself feeling upset about some little thing like someone being later than they thought they would be, or feeling left out when I think I should be included, I just start repeating the mantra and soon it all seems unimportant and the situation passes without a major confrontation which would have been the result in the past.

And more often than not, the person who I would have been mad at, rather than being on the defensive and trying to justify what happened, ends up explaining and apologizing if that is appropriate. The result for me is better relationships and a more relaxed way of living.

Alex: Calmer Meetings

When I first started doing mantra, it was difficult to get in the mood because it took so much concentration and focus, but with daily practice and the desire for its results, I got better at it. It helped quiet my mind and helped me realize that I could manage my new responsibilities at my job effectively and successfully. My director and co-workers noticed the difference.

At our first couple of meetings they noticed that I was nervous and anxious. Now I am more relaxed and at ease when I lead the meetings. They've commented on this. Using the mantra has helped me develop a calmer disposition at my meetings and **enjoy** my new responsibilities.

Mantra has the power to transform your life in an almost miraculous way if you let it work for you. In helping you stay more in the here-and-now, it allows you to experience the world as less stressful. When good things happen to you, you can enjoy them completely. When undesirable things happen, you can more easily accept that they've happened and go on with life instead of using energy to deny or resist these events that have already happened. And since it is a relatively simple technique that can be done at almost any time or place, it is an excellent way to experience that you **do** have the power to transform your life in a positive, beneficial, and healthy way.

7

Feel Better And Make Your Load Easier To Carry By...........

Exercising Regularly

You may be just about to skip over this section because you've been hearing all your life about the benefits of physical exercise, and you don't really want to hear any more about it. Well, do yourself a favor — read this and think one more time about the benefits of regular exercise. It may surprise you, but one of the best things you can do for yourself if you want to live a more relaxed life is to make a commitment to frequent physical exercise. An exercise routine will improve your physical and emotional well-being, as well as strengthening your ability to cope with the stresses of your daily life.

EXERCISERS ARE HEALTHIER AND HAPPIER

According to data we've collected from adults who have completed our Computerized Stress Inventory in doctor's offices, counseling centers or wellness programs around the country, people who exercise regularly are twice as likely as non- exercisers to feel very satisfied with life. We've also found that people who **do not** exercise regularly are three times more likely to feel very unsatisfied with life than are people who do routine exercise.

Our data also show that adults who engage in regular exercise are two-and-a-half times more likely than inactive adults to say they almost always have fun in their lives. People who do not exercise regularly are three times more likely than exercisers to say they seldom or almost never have fun in their lives. Similarly, a recent Gallup poll found that adults who exercise regularly are two-and-a-half times more likely than non-exercisers to say they are happy.

The Gallup Poll also described positive changes people reported in their lives since beginning regular exercise. About half reported that they felt sick less often than usual since they started exercising and that they now have less stress on the job and in their personal lives. More than one in three said they are more creative at work and feel better about their careers. Over 60% claimed to have experienced a major surge in energy.

The effects of regular exercise on preventing and combatting heart disease, high blood pressure and osteoporosis (progressive bone deterioration) are well-known. Scientists today report that maintaining a moderate exercise regimen can significantly increase life expectancy and improve one's quality of life.

Studies have shown that people on regular exercise programs tend to:

- be more healthy,
- have better vital capacity,
- handle problems better,
- sleep better,
- cope with life more satisfactorily, feel better,
- be more optimistic, and
- have a better self-image.

MAKING THE EXERCISE DECISION

Even though the benefits of regular exercise are widely publicized, less than half the adult population in the United States exercises as much as the recommended three 20-minute sessions a week, according to a Centers for Disease Control national survey. The CDC concluded that promotion of exercise should be a national priority.

In our workshops we generally find people are resistant to the idea of exercising on a regular basis. They usually say they just don't have the time for exercise, or they don't have the equipment, or they are just too tired. Interestingly, surveys have shown that when people do begin exercising they usually do it because they have decided they are out of shape or overweight or are worried about getting that way. Even though exercise is known to reduce stress, people don't generally seem to turn to it for stress relief, but rather discover that benefit as an unexpected byproduct.

In each workshop we find a couple of people who for some reason have been pushed into exercising regularly, and who report that to their surprise exercise has completely transformed their lives. Nancy's story is a typical example:

Nancy: I Wish I'd Started Sooner

I still find it hard to believe that I am doing aerobic exercise! One thing I do know, though — if I can do it, anyone can. I'm sure I'm the last person anyone would have expected to be doing this. I've never been physically fit in my life — my grade school didn't have P.E., and even in junior high and high school I only had about three years of it.

I've always been terrible at all sports — the last one to get chosen for the baseball team as a kid, always finishing last in races — that sort of thing. Frankly, I avoided physical activity as much as I could. When I was in college, I had to take P.E. for a year, so I took tennis and almost flunked because I almost never could hit the ball over the net. This may sound like an exaggeration, but believe me, it's true! ...

I never felt any real need to exercise because I was always thin, even when I ate whatever I wanted, and I was unaware of any benefits of exercise beyond weight control. It absolutely never occurred to me that I could actually **feel** better if I exercised.

Then I got into my thirties and started to put on a little weight. I love cooking and eating what I cook, as well as eating out, so I find it difficult to stick to a diet very long. I began to consider exercise as a possibility. At the same time, people all over the country were getting involved in jogging and other types of aerobic exercise, and lots of new books and articles were coming out on the subject. ...

So I took the plunge! I bought a good exercise bicycle and Kenneth Cooper's books on aerobic exercise. I started slowly and gradually worked up to a program where I ride the bicycle for twenty-five minutes a day, six days a week, at a tension level and speed which keeps my pulse at the required rate for aerobic exercise. I'm not saying it's easy. Even now, after I've been riding for a few minutes, I feel like I'll never finish the whole twenty-five minutes. But then I get into the rhythm of it and it kind of flows along. Also, I watch TV while I ride, which keeps my mind occupied. I considered jogging, but knew I wouldn't do it when the weather was bad, so the bicycle is better for me. ...

Anyway, what's amazing is how much better I feel! I definitely have more energy now, and I feel much better about my body and more interested in getting involved in other physical activity. I hardly ever get the stiff necks and backaches I used to get so often. What really surprises me is how relaxed I feel when I finish riding and how this feeling stays with me all through the day. If I am away for a few days and don't ride, I actually miss it. My figure has firmed up, my clothes fit better, and I can keep my weight at a normal level more easily. I don't think I'll ever give up regular exercise now that I've finally discovered it — I only wish it had happened sooner!

HOW MUCH EXERCISE IS ENOUGH?

If you are not already exercising on a regular basis, it is important that you at least consider changing your lifestyle enough that you can include exercise several times a week. Research shows, and experts agree that the real key to using exercise to reduce tension is to exercise **regularly.** The once-a- week basketball game doesn't do it, but there are many enjoyable activities that do.

There are two types of physical exercise that are particularly useful for reducing stress and tension:

1. **Vigorous, aerobic exercise:** Jogging, Bicycling, Swimming, Skating, Rowing, Aerobic Dance, Brisk Walking, Handball, etc.

   The key is to elevate your heart rate to between 60 and 80 percent of its maximum level (subtract your age from 220 and multiply the result by 60% and 80% to get your range) long enough and often enough to get the benefits. Generally if you exercise at the heart rates at the lower end of the range, you should do it longer and for more days per week. For example, a brisk 45- minute walk, four to five days a week gives similar results to a 20 to 30-minute run three to four days a week.

2. **Stretching exercises:** Yoga and other muscle-stretching exercises.

   These stretching and toning exercises are usually done for 30 to 40 minutes a day five or six days a week. Focus is on slow-motion stretching movements that increase flexibility. These exercises do not improve cardio-vascular fitness, but can provide all the other benefits of regular exercise.

BENEFITS OF REGULAR EXERCISE

Each of these types of exercise is a useful part of a stress management plan. Each has benefits. Benefits you can expect to get from **either** type of exercise when you exercise regularly:

- You feel more relaxed in general, and you find you can relax more easily. Exercise reduces tension when you are doing it, and leaves you in a calmer, more relaxed state.

- You sleep better.

- You feel energetic rather than weary and fatigued.

- You can control your body weight more easily — and without drastic dieting. This helps you feel better about your appearance, which also improves your self-esteem.

- Your muscle tone improves, your skin is more firm, and your body is more flexible. You get rid of stiffness and flabbiness.

- You feel more alert and have a more positive attitude. You feel better about yourself and more in control of your life.

- Your blood circulation improves and this increases the health and strength of vital organs and glands. You are healthier, get sick less frequently, and generally feel better.

We cannot teach you **how** to exercise here. We can only remind you that physical exercise is an important part of your life. To learn specific types of exercise, we recommend that you either enroll in an exercise class, or read one of the books on exercise we list at the end of this book. Of course if you have been involved in some exercise program before, you can resume it again. Before beginning any exercise program, however, you should consider the following points.

IMPORTANT POINTS TO REMEMBER

✔ If you are beginning an exercise program, it is best to have a complete physical examination before you start, particularly if you are over 35, overweight, or have been ill. Discuss the exercise plan you have chosen with your doctor to be sure that type of exercise is suitable for you.

✔ Choose an exercise program that offers you something to look forward to — plan to exercise with friends, run or walk in a beautiful area, join a class or health club. You'll be more likely to stick to a program you enjoy.

✔ Work into your exercise program gradually, so that your body can get used to new levels of activity. Don't try to compete or break records. Adjust your exercise to **you.** The idea is not to do as much as you can as fast as you can, it is to gradually increase your capacity for exercise.

✔ Exercise regularly, several times each week.

✔ Remember that an exercise program takes will power. If it were easy to exercise regularly, most people would be doing it already.

You will be tempted to skip exercise days or give up. The best way to get into exercising regularly is to **promise yourself** that you will stick to your exercise plan for eight weeks without letting yourself out of it. By the end of that time, you'll be enjoying the way you feel and won't want to quit.

Jim's experience is a good example:

Jim: Former Couch Potato

I'm glad this project motivated me to take up exercise again. When I was in school I got a lot of exercise but since I graduated and started working full-time, I hadn't been. My typical pattern when I got home from work was to flop myself on the sofa, eat a snack, watch some television, and sometimes take a nap. When I took naps, I ended up even more tired than before. The more sleep I got, the more drowsy and disengaged I became. ...

When I started this stress-management program, I decided I would do stretching exercises and jog after I got home from work. At first, though, I would come home and be tempted to lay around. I would think to myself, "Boy, I'm so tired. I want to take a nap." But most of the time I would put on my running clothes, do some exercises and go jogging.

When I got home I was always much more energized. I realized that I got energy by giving out energy.

I started out jogging one-half mile and gradually increased the distance. I'm now up to two miles. I do the stretching exercises daily and jog five to six days a week. I started nine weeks ago.....

I've learned that fatigue is a state of mind and a matter of recycling energy. The honest truth is that hard work does not produce fatigue, and rest does not alleviate fatigue. I've also learned that my relationship with myself is a vital factor in my energy level. If I feel good about myself—which I do when I exercise—then I have more vitality and power.

8

Feel Better And Make Your Load Easier To Carry By...........

Eating For Good Health

You've probably heard the old expression, "You are what you eat." There's a lot of wisdom in those words. In fact, what you eat does make a great deal of difference in the way you feel. People who eat well-balanced diets are generally healthier and better able to cope with stress than are people who eat less well.

FOODS AND MOODS

Research has demonstrated a connection between food and moodiness, although as yet studies have not been able to pinpoint particular foods as the source of certain moods. Among adults who have completed our *Computerized Stress Inventory,* those who eat a variety of foods each day, who do not often skip meals, and/or who do not frequently snack on sweets report less stress and more satisfaction with life than those whose eating habits are less healthy.

Investigators have also discovered links between vitamins and stress, but they emphasize that an adequate diet is a better source of needed nutrients than are vitamin supplements. In fact, supplements can lead to overdoses of vitamins stored in the body. Well-chosen nutrition, on the other hand, gives your body the materials it needs to cope with stress.

FOODS AND HEALTH

Most of us already know what we need to eat to feel good and stay healthy. To refresh your memory, the U.S. Department of Agriculture recommends a diet that includes a variety of foods each day, including selections of:

- Fruits,
- Vegetables,
- Whole grain products, enriched breads, and cereals,
- Milk, cheese and yogurt,
- Meats, poultry, fish, eggs,
- Legumes (dry peas and beans).

The U.S.D.A. also recommends:

- Limiting fat (especially saturated fat) and cholesterol,
- Avoiding excess sugar and salt,
- Eating the majority of daily calories from complex carbohydrate foods (vegetables, fruits, grains, beans, etc.).

PROBLEM EATING HABITS

In spite of all the publicity about nutrition, health surveys tell us that American eating habits have not improved much in the last ten years. Our research results also indicate that large numbers of American adults have unhealthy eating patterns. Among those who have taken our *Computerized Stress Inventory,* 55% report eating sweet snacks between meals more than three times a week, 44% say they often skip meals, 36% drink more than five cups of caffeinated beverages a day, 65% eat when they are bored, and 57% say they often feel heavy or sleepy after meals.

The problem most of us have is not that we don't know what we should eat, it is that we don't know what we **do** eat. We eat meals in restaurants or grab a snack in a rush or just generally eat in an unplanned way without thinking about whether we are getting the nutrients we need.

Another problem with eating in an unplanned way is that we give too little attention to **when** we eat. For example, we may skip breakfast because we are rushed in the morning or simply want to get a few extra minutes of sleep. Trying to save time by skipping breakfast is like trying to save money by not putting any money in the parking meter. The fine you end up paying is a lot more than you originally saved. The fine we pay for missing breakfast shows up as lowered work output, lack of energy, or feeling tense and irritable. Furthermore, research indicates that a nutritionally poor breakfast, or black coffee alone, is even worse than no breakfast at all.

If you don't eat breakfast, it is harder to get your day's quota of essential nutrients. Also, it is more likely that you will be tempted to eat mid-morning "coffee break" snacks, such as donuts and sweet rolls, which are high in calories but do little to meet your nutritional needs. You will get a good start on the day if you eat a breakfast that supplies you with about one fourth of your daily requirements for calories, protein, and other needed nutrients. Remember that breakfast doesn't need to consist of traditional breakfast foods, as long as it's nourishing.

Eating in an unplanned way may also mean that most of your eating is in the form of snacks rather than meals. This can be fine, or it can be a problem, depending on what you eat in your snacks. Snacks between meals can be useful in giving you extra energy when you need it, and in controlling hunger and helping you eat less at meals. It is important to remember, though, that snacks are a part of your day's intake of food, and should contribute nutrition as well as calories. You can even eat nutritiously by eating **only** snacks if you pay attention and plan what you eat to meet your daily requirements. The key is to be aware of what you are eating and choose healthy foods.

AN EXPERIMENT TO TRY

If you would like to become more aware of what you eat and how it affects you, try an experiment. For a week, write down everything you eat each day and what time of day you eat it (including all snacks, coffee, and alcoholic drinks). Also, at the end of each day, write a sentence or two about how you felt in general during that day. If you can remember, also include a note about what times of day you felt best and what times you felt worst. At the end of the week, take a look at what you have written and ask yourself these questions:

1. How well does what I eat each day supply me with the foods I need for a healthy diet?

2. Can I perceive any connection between what I ate or drank on a given day and how I felt that day? Or between **when** I ate or drank and how I felt?

Now, for the next two weeks, experiment. Continue writing down everything you eat each day and what time of day you eat it, but eat differently than you did before. If you haven't been eating foods from all the recommended groups, try that. If you've been eating or drinking an excess of something, such as sweets, coffee, or fried foods, cut down or eliminate these foods for two weeks. If you've been eating several heavy meals each day, eat more lightly. If you've been skipping breakfast, eat breakfast. Again, write down how you've been feeling at the end of each day.

At the end of the two weeks, look at what you've written down and compare it to the first week, when you were eating your usual way. Ask yourself these questions:

1. When I eat differently, do I feel differently? If so, do I feel better or worse?

2. Would I like to make some changes in my eating habits?

PROBLEMS TO WATCH FOR

This experiment is designed to get you to start paying attention to your body, to find out how you feel after you eat different foods, eat different amounts of food, or eat at different times than you normally do. Pay particular attention to the following specific problems or foods:

Sugar: Sugar gives you quick energy because it is rapidly converted into glucose, which then enters your bloodstream. However, you also quickly produce insulin to metabolize the sugar. This causes your glucose level to drop rapidly, which may make you feel tired or dizzy. Frequent high-sugar snacks during the day may keep your energy level going up and down like a yo-yo.

Fiber: Many nutritionists believe that the modern diet with its high content of refined foods does not provide us with the fiber we need. Fiber, the part of the food we eat that is not digested or absorbed by our bodies, helps keep our system running smoothly. If you aren't getting enough fiber, you may be frequently constipated — and this is definitely a source of stress! Consider increasing your intake of fresh fruits and vegetables, and whole grain breads and cereals. Eat a high-fiber bran cereal for breakfast. You may be amazed at how much better you feel!

Caffeine: The caffeine in coffee, cola drinks and tea is a stimulant. It can give you a quick pickup, but since the energy boost will only last about 90 minutes, you'll be tempted to keep going back for more. You will probably find that you will feel more relaxed during the day and sleep better at night if you do not consume large quantities of caffeine. Experts recommend two or three cups of coffee a day at most. Find out how caffeine affects you. Don's experience is an example:

> By keeping the log on my behavior and food consumption, I see a direct correlation between caffeine and sleeplessness. I have the continual struggle with loving the taste of good coffee and the

> "buzz" of caffeine and the difficulty I have had relaxing. I continually vacillate from no use to abuse. I definitely do not have this problem under control yet, but I am well aware of the consequences of caffeine.

Overeating: We live in a land of plenty, which is obvious when looking at our expanding waistlines. Obesity is one of the greatest health hazards in America today. Eat well, but don't overeat. You will feel better, stay healthier, and live longer.

A NOTE ABOUT CHANGE

Any type of change in your daily routines is a challenge. Changing eating habits is particularly difficult. Be prepared for some setbacks if you are trying to cut back or give up favorite foods. If you do slip, don't see it as total failure and an indication that you can't change your eating patterns. Simply realize that it is an indication that your goal is not an easy one. Also, notice what led to the slip and look for ways to avoid such situations in the future.

Since human nature tends to crave what it can't have, deciding to completely eliminate a specific food or type of food may be setting yourself up for failure. Remember that cutting back is still progress and that the most lasting changes are usually made gradually.

You will probably find certain times of day or circumstances bring about strong urges to go back to your old eating habits. When that happens, try distracting yourself with an activity that doesn't involve eating, or snack on a healthy substitute food.

The next example shows how these techniques worked for one person as she made some major changes in her eating patterns.

Kim: Fewer Sweets, More Energy

> I felt that Eating Right was a good exercise for me to begin to work on. I knew this would be hard for me because I have a real sweet tooth that is constantly my downfall. I enjoy eating almost anything with sugar; sometimes I turn things down because they aren't rich and chocolatey enough for me and I know I can find something better if I keep looking. This affects my regular eating because I am often too full from sweet snacks to eat a meal, so I just pick at things or skip the meal entirely. Then of course I end up snacking on something else because I can't make it until the next meal.
>
> I knew that staying away from sugar for 8 weeks would be hard but I felt like I was getting to the point where I could no longer keep slowly starving my body of nourishment without having some

long-term effects. I also knew that I would not only have to stop eating sugar but start eating things that were good for me. ...

I started the process of retraining myself in regard to my eating habits knowing that I would probably have some small setbacks along the way, but that I could always begin again. I couldn't expect myself to make a complete turnover on demand, but I was hoping for good results and was determined to see myself through the 8-week period.

I had begun noticing articles on the effects of sugar on the body and was observing some patterns in myself. One thing was the way I had headaches in the evenings, probably from the sugar I had eaten. I also noticed that at times I would feel weak and shaky like I was about to pass out. ...

To begin my new way of eating, one of the things I forced myself to do was to eat breakfast. I like all kinds of foods (but had cut them out in favor of sugar), so I knew it would be no trouble to find foods I liked — it was just hard to change my habits. For breakfast I ate a bran cereal low in sugar or made some bran muffins at home. I also drank some milk, which I hadn't been drinking since I was a kid, or some juice.

This stopped me from feeling hungry and I didn't feel the same kind of temptation to eat a doughnut to get me through to lunch as I had so often done before. I was also then hungry when it was time for lunch. I ate a variety of non-greasy things for lunch, usually salad and maybe some fish, chicken or turkey.

The afternoons were much more profitable as far as working and feeling more alert because I had eaten well but lightly. Usually I brought a piece of fruit for an afternoon snack to get me through to dinner. ...

I began to enjoy cooking and eating regular dinners with vegetables, salad and meat, fish or chicken. The hard habit to break was evening sweets and snacking, but with fruit for snacks and keeping myself busy, I began to get out of the habit and not crave sweets. ...

The first few weeks were the hardest because I felt few results and it was a constant battle with myself to refrain from "treats." But as time went by and I realized I could say no to myself, I felt a certain pride in what I was doing. And, I no longer had headaches at bedtime.

The next change I noticed was in my general energy level. First, in the mornings after eating breakfast I was more cheerful with people. By the third or fourth week I was able to get a lot more done. Time went by more quickly because I wasn't hungry.

Then in the third or fourth week I felt the change in the way I felt in the afternoons. I wasn't sleepy or hungry and again time went by much more quickly. I felt better all over, had more energy, and wasn't as irritable or crabby. I found work more pleasant and rewarding and my co-workers appeared to be more pleasant and relaxed (probably because I was more pleasant to them.) ...

Physically my body feels better. I don't get so many aches and pains as I used to. Changing my diet has clearly added to my personal enjoyment and quality of life. I feel proud that I was able to do this for myself, and I plan to continue eating this way.

9

Feel Better And Make Your Load Easier To Carry By............

Expanding Your Awareness

Although it may seem to be a strange idea, one way to improve the quality of your life is to think about your death. We are all going to die; our time in this existence is finite. However, we have a tendency not to think about this — even to the extent that we don't really accept our own mortality. This may seem natural, but actually it's a denial of our nature. By not letting ourselves recognize and accept that our time here is limited, we conceal from ourselves the value of our time, which is a precious resource. We sometimes find ourselves wishing away time, or merely passing time, rather than really living. We don't appreciate or really experience what is going on around us and inside us.

LESSONS FROM THE DYING

People who work with the dying say they learn some valuable lessons from them. Particularly, they learn to live in the present. People who are facing death focus on the little things — nature, the seasons, a beautiful sunset — and they really experience these. They don't put things off. Many put more living into a few months or a year than some of us do in a lifetime.

We don't have to wait until we are dying to learn to appreciate living. We can choose to experience more of our lives right now, rather than waiting until we are actually confronted with a "now or never" situation. By learning to take advantage of all the beauty and pleasure available to us in our daily lives, we can begin to enjoy life a great deal more. We find ourselves feeling more calm and relaxed, happier, and more capable of coping with the problems that come up in our lives.

LIVING IN THE MOMENT

To fully enjoy the pleasure and beauty in your life, you must expand your awareness. Often you are unable to really be in the present because your mind is focused on the future or the past, rather than on the moment. For example, if you are eating a fragrant, juicy orange, and at the same time are worrying about a phone call you have to make, or the argument you had with a friend yesterday, you are missing most of the pleasure you could be getting from the orange. You could be focusing on the delicious smell and taste of that orange, but instead you are almost unaware of the orange as you focus on your worries.

Here are some other examples of ways we cheat ourselves from experiencing the present:

- Walking without seeing what's around us;
- Overlooking the change of seasons;
- Hearing music without really paying attention;
- Listening to someone without really hearing;
- Working on a project while focusing only on getting the job done.

You can change this by teaching yourself to put your attention on what you are doing. Put your worries aside for a while. If you are washing the dishes, try doing it the way a young child would by enjoying the feeling of the soap and warm water on your hands and the sparkling look of the clean dishes. As long as you are going to do the dishes anyway, you may as well let that job serve you as a relaxing break rather than wishing you didn't have to take the time to do it in the first place.

If you are walking along the street remind yourself to be aware of yourself walking, to be aware of the wind or the sun, to be aware of the sights and sounds around you. By doing this you can arrive at your destination relaxed and refreshed. Awareness helps you stay calm and alert.

When you truly open yourself to the moment this way, you find happiness right in front of you. You suddenly discover that nothing has to go right for you to be happy, you just have to decide to enjoy what you are doing.

ACTIVITIES TO EXPAND AWARENESS

Here are some activities to help you expand your awareness of the present. Once you have tried these you will be able to come up with plenty of new ones.

1. Eating Fruit. Choose a piece of fruit. An orange is especially good because of its spicy odor, but an apple, grape, peach, or pear will do. A strawberry would be terrific! Now take the fruit and sit down in a quiet place. Hold the fruit in your hands, turn it around, feel its weight and texture. See how it reflects light. Take some time to smell the fruit and enjoy the fragrance. Look carefully at the fruit, and observe its form, size, and color. Peel the fruit, if that is necessary before you can eat it. Now you are ready to taste the fruit. Close your eyes and slowly take a bite. Let yourself fully experience the taste. Now, slowly finish eating the fruit, and while you are eating, let yourself be aware of the pleasure you are getting from the experience.

2. Being With Someone. Take 10 or 15 minutes to sit down with someone and talk. This person might be your wife or husband, your child, a friend, a relative. While you are with this person, don't be doing anything else — just be with the person. Let yourself really look at the person, really **see** him or her, and experience how much you really care about this person. This doesn't need to be a heavy conversation. Just talk about whatever interests you both. Be aware of the other person and really **hear** what he or she is saying. If you find yourself thinking about what you will say next instead of listening to the other person, remind yourself to be **aware** of the person you are talking with. Enjoy yourself and experience the pleasure you are getting from just being together.

Exercises such as these will allow you to realize the potential for joy that is present in all the activities of your daily life. You can practice expanding your awareness of the present as you simply go about the business of living. Because you are probably not in the habit of experiencing your life this way, it might be difficult at first. But, if you keep working on it you will find that it becomes easier to see and fully enjoy what is around you — and you will find the rewards tremendous.

You may find that you feel a little guilty at taking this pleasure in life when you live in such a serious problem-filled world. If you do, ask yourself whether maintaining your own gloomy, worried or rushed attitude will really help to make the world a better place. Remember, happiness is contagious and you can pass along to others the joy you find around you.

HOW THIS TECHNIQUE WORKS FOR OTHERS

The process of learning to expand your awareness, and the benefits from doing so, will be clearer when you hear how this technique has worked for others.

Carole: Richer On The Inside

I was at a very low point in my life when I first learned these awareness exercises. I felt depressed and overwhelmed by the immensity of my responsibility as a working single parent, and in despair at the meagerness of my strength. I felt alone — unable to give or receive anything meaningful.

Practicing the awareness exercises had a startling effect on me. I was bombarded with sensations and realizations. It had been so long since I had felt the hot soapy water, been aware of the texture of the dish cloth, and felt the smooth clean surface of the cleaned plate. As I concentrated on all these sensations, I was aware of other thoughts tugging at my mind — "I should plan the work schedule for the kids"; "If you start the laundry now, It will be done when the dishes are done." I realized that much of the time I had been trying to do three things at the same time! That was supposed to justify my existence or increase my value as a person. ...

Being efficient and getting lots of things done quickly certainly have merit, but when my whole life seemed to demand that intensity of activity, there was never any time to tune in to what was going on right now. As I began to slow down and be aware of what I was doing, feeling, and saying, and of what was going on around me at the moment, I found I could listen easier, concentrate better, and understand more quickly. It was easier for me to "be" with my kids and my friends.

Now I feel richer on the inside. My sense are sharpened, colors are brighter, sounds clearer, tastes and smells more satisfying. I have noticed that I spend more time hugging my kids (something that I always felt I "should" do but was somehow difficult). Now it came naturally and is very enjoyable. It isn't something I do or make happen. It's just there. I don't feel so alone with my kids.

Larry: Experience Every Moment

It is very difficult for me to practice awareness, but I'm struggling along, taking one step at a time. So much of my life has been spent hurrying from one place to another, ignoring everything that happens in between. Another problem is that once I reach my destination, I often continue to think of what's ahead instead of focusing my attention on the present. I'm finally realizing that I'm letting life slip by without experiencing it in its totality.

Now, when I'm walking alone I try to say to myself, "I have just taken a step and it's great to be alive". While I'm doing this I also like to look around, to be more aware of where I am and how beautiful everything really is. I've also been trying to carry this over to my other activities. For example, when I'm sitting in a meeting, I think to myself, "I'm here, I feel relaxed, and there is no place I'd rather be."

I am learning how to "be" with other people when I am with them. I work on keeping eye contact with the person, staying in the present, and experiencing right in that moment all that I can about that person — really listening and tuning in to all the things they are communicating. This practice is not easy. It takes more concentrating, more energy, and more time. I do find though, that the more I practice, the more aware I become. And the rewards are great as I experience myself and my relationships with others more fully. It's like we're each discovering the other again. ...

I find it challenging and exciting to have the opportunity to expand my awareness of life and its specialness. Even though keeping myself aware is difficult, the effects are truly remarkable. The way I feel now is that I don't want to let a moment go by without enjoying it, because I can never have that moment back again. To me, the saddest thing in life would be to come to the end and realize that I never really experienced life itself.

Michelle: Feeling Like A Child Again

Before I practiced this technique I was extremely caught up in my busy schedule. I felt overwhelmed. All I thought of was what I had to do. Today I am still very busy, but at least once a day I make a conscious effort to experience a new awareness.

I have had many wonderful experiences. For example, one cool fall day when I was out walking, auburn leaves were falling off the trees and floating through the air. I stopped and watched them drift. Then I sat in the leaves, listened to them crunch, and felt them. I was aware of the pleasure I got out of this experience. What a renewing and joyful adventure that was! ...

Since I have started working on expanding my awareness, I personally can tell a difference in how I interact with others and with my environment. Since I am usually a positive person, no one has told me they have noticed a difference in me, but I know I am different. When I expand my awareness it makes me feel like a child again. I feel more sensitized, stimulated, alert and enthusiastic! I am seeing the world and its beauty through different eyes and it sure makes living more meaningful.

A month ago I discovered a lump in my neck that gave me a tremendous scare. Luckily, it was not abnormal, but it certainly made me think about death. It made me realize that our time is limited, and that if we don't appreciate and really experience what is going on around us and inside us then we are not fully living.

YOUR CHALLENGE

Don't wait for a life-threatening scare. Wake up to the world around you today. Experiences like the ones these people describe are available to you whenever you choose to take the time for them. They don't cost anything, they don't have undesirable side effects, and they give you the best that life has to offer — the experience of living. Let yourself be aware — experience now!

10

Feel Better And Make Your Load Easier To Carry By...........

Using Imagery

We each have a remarkable ability that can allow us to easily exceed what we have accepted as the limits of our everyday lives. We can go to places that are far away, be with people who are not near us, even feel ourselves being completely different than we are now — all through imagery. Our minds have this creative ability and we can use it for many purposes.

YOUR NATURAL POWER OF IMAGINATION

We all know we have this ability because we have dreams in which we find ourselves in places we have never been, doing things we have never done. As a child you may have played "pretend," but as an adult you may have forgotten just how relaxing and how much fun it can be to use your imagination. It can also help you make your life more profitable and satisfying.

Before you try using imagery you may have to overcome some negative feelings about it.

- You may call it daydreaming, and think of it as wasting time, or as an escape, a useless activity.

- You may believe that imagining yourself achieving great success is vain or conceited.

- You may find it frightening to imagine something very different from your daily life — like imagining yourself to be a tree or animal, or being in a foreign country. Somehow this may seem unnatural, or you may feel afraid that if you do this you won't be able to get back to the way you were.

- You may be afraid other people will find out about your fantasies and you will be embarrassed. What if they think you are crazy or stupid?

Actually it is good for you to let yourself go and enjoy your ability to fantasize — provided you don't overdo it and start spending most of your time this way. Recent psychological findings reveal that "creative imagining" is important for good mental health and can be one of our most constructive mental activities. We should cultivate this ability.

Most people do daydream almost every day. These imaginings though are rarely planned and are often even negative scenes where we see ourselves failing at a task or ending up in an embarrassing situation. This sort of imagery adds to our stress rather than relieving it. With a little practice, daydreaming sessions can easily turn into a force for effective change in your life.

BENEFITS OF IMAGERY

Imagery releases creative energy and enhances ingenuity and original thinking. In addition, you can:

- Explore the world vicariously through imagery. Imagining yourself in another place, time, or lifestyle helps you better understand the world, yourself, and others.

- Give yourself a mental break by imagining yourself on a warm, sunny beach; or maybe on a snowy mountaintop. By withdrawing from a tense situation briefly, you get some rest and support. You come back with more energy.

- Rehearse a situation that you expect to be unpleasant. Imagine yourself coping easily with the situation so that everything works out as you want it to. This helps you get in touch with your inner power.

- Relive your past successes to give your self-esteem a boost when you need it.

- Solve a difficult problem you are wrestling with by letting your mind drift. Your unconscious can often provide the answer.

- Relieve anger and frustration by replaying an upsetting scene but changing the outcome to be more desirable.

- Practice athletic, musical or other skills without actually performing the activity. Many top athletes perfect their performances by mentally going through the moves in their minds.

ACTIVITIES FOR USING IMAGERY

To give you some practice in using imagery, and some ideas you may not have thought about, we are including some imagery activities here for you to try. Read the instructions through first and then let go and see where your imagination takes you. After you have tried these, you will be able to think of many others. Also, some of the books recommended at the end of this book, particularly those by Stevens and by Huxley, contain many other imagery activities you will enjoy.

Relaxing Imagery. Lie down or sit in a comfortable position. Mentally go through all the parts of your body and let go of any tension you feel while doing this. Close your eyes and relax. Take several deep breaths, letting each one out slowly. Now ... imagine you are on a beautiful warm sunny beach ... or in a cool shady forest ... or anywhere you can completely relax. Let yourself experience the sounds that you hear and the way you feel lying or sitting there. Just be there and enjoy yourself. If thoughts of problems or worries come up, just notice them and let them drift by. Don't let these thoughts intrude into your relaxing place. Stay in your relaxing place until you feel calm and ready to return. When you are ready to come back, say goodbye to your relaxing place, knowing that you can return whenever you want to. Now, slowly begin to stretch your muscles, and when you are ready open your eyes and return to today.

Creative Imagery. Lie or sit comfortably, relax, and take deep breaths as instructed in the beginning of the relaxing imagery. Close your eyes and imagine that you are your favorite animal. Experience how you feel being this animal. Are you large or small? What do you look like? Imagine that you, as this animal, are walking around the place where you live. How does your world look? Where do you get your food, and what do you eat? What is your life like? How do you spend your time? When you have finished exploring your experience as this animal, imagine yourself back in your present form in your own world. Slowly begin to move around and when you are ready, return to today. Because this type of fantasy stimulates creativity, you may want to draw a picture or write out your experiences. It is also fun to do this imagery with other people and then talk about your experiences with each other afterward. You will be amazed at how unique and creative each person's imagery is.

Success Imagery. Lie or sit comfortably, relax, and take deep breaths, as instructed in the beginning of the relaxing imagery. Think of some activity you'd like to do better (maybe playing tennis or singing), or of some desired outcome in your life (maybe getting a job, solving a problem, or finding enough money to do something you want to do). Now, close your eyes and imagine this aspect of your life going exactly as you want it to go. Actually see yourself playing that terrific game of tennis, or singing on stage. Watch yourself working out your problems easily, or finding the money you need with no problem. See how relaxed you are ... feel your self-confidence as you move through this activity. Know that you can do this easily whenever you want to. Enjoy experiencing yourself as this successful, confident, relaxed person. When you are ready, slowly begin to move around, open your eyes and return to today.

Communicating Imagery. Again, lie or sit comfortably, relax, and take deep breaths, as instructed in the beginning of the relaxing imagery. Close you eyes and think of someone you have a conflict with, or someone you would like to talk to about something. Imagine that you and that person are together in a very comfortable place talking. Tell the person you are glad to have the chance to talk. Look at the person in your imagination and listen to what he or she says to you. Now ... tell that person what you really want to tell him or her. What does that person say back to you? Imagine that you are really able to understand this person ... to know how he or she feels. Now you know just what to say to this person so that things will be clear between you, and you will feel relaxed and comfortable together. Say what you want to say to this person, and listen to what he or she says to you. When you have finished the conversation, say goodbye and prepare to return to today. Slowly move your body and open your eyes when you are ready.

CREATE YOUR OWN IMAGERIES

Now that you know how to use imagery, the possibilities are unlimited. You can choose other relaxing places, creative possibilities, or ways of solving problems. For example, imagine you are a tree in a forest, or a person of another race, or are living in another country. Or imagine yourself doing something you have always wanted to do —

climbing a mountain, dancing, or running your own business — and imagine yourself doing it well.

A young man we know used this technique to help him in his search for a job. His qualifications were good, so he was easily able to get to the point of being invited in for job interviews. The problem was that he believed that the job situation was so competitive that other applicants were more qualified, so he was unable to relax and present himself in a calm, self-confident manner in interviews.

We suggested to him that he try a short imagery exercise several times a day before each new interview. He was to relax, close his eyes, and imagine himself as vividly as possible at the job interview. He would "see" himself calmly, confidently answering questions. He would "feel" the friendly atmosphere between himself and the interviewer. He would "hear" the interviewer telling him that he was exactly the person they had been looking for. He would imagine the happy ending of getting just the job he wanted, and he would feel this to the best of his ability.

The young man did this exercise so often that he soon began to expect himself to present himself well in interviews and to anticipate that the outcome would be as he desired. In a few weeks he had a job he liked and the satisfaction of knowing that he had gotten it using his own inner strength.

DEVELOP THE POWER OF YOUR IMAGINATION

Even though using imagery is a natural activity, most of us have spent a lot of time suppressing it, believing that fantasy does not fit with learning to live in the 'real' world. So, it might take a little time to feel comfortable daydreaming on purpose. If you do give yourself permission to try these exercises regularly, you may be surprised at the results. Marge's experience is a good example:

Marge: Multiple Uses Of Imagery

I have never thought of myself as a creative person. I believe that as children enter school their creativity is squelched in an effort to make them conform. This part of my socialization was well accomplished. Furthermore I can remember the ridicule to which I was subjected at home when I played "fantasy" games. The message was that not only were the things I did strange, but that I was strange for doing them. In my family, or at least to me, strange meant bad.

I knew using imagery would be a challenge. but felt that it might be a useful skill for me to master. I began using imagery several days a week and learned to enjoy the escape it could provide.

I especially enjoyed "visiting" relaxing places such as a sunny beach, a cool forest, or a wind-blown mountaintop. Over time I found myself better able to "feel" all the sensations a place offered such as the warm sun on my skin or the wind in my face; to "hear" the birds calling or the surf breaking; and to "smell" the salt air or the musty dampness of vegetation. It seemed as though noticing these things in my fantasies made me more aware of them as I went through my day so that things I usually took for granted were experienced with a renewed delight—a very rewarding experience. ...

I also found imagery useful in my work. For example, one day I had an important meeting to request funding for several projects for my unit. I took time the day before and that day to imagine myself presenting my proposals in a confident, self-assured manner. Further, I imagined some objections my boss might raise and the replies I would give. Finally, I imagined my response as he approved or disapproved each proposal.

This worked very well for me. I did a good job of presenting my requests, responded well to his questions and concerns regarding some of them, and was able to calmly accept his decision to fund some proposals but not others. In the past, I've had a hard time accepting rejection of any proposals without feeling like a failure. Imagining the meeting helped me to act more professionally because I wasn't focused just on getting what I thought my unit needed. Since I had gone through the conversation in my imagination, I was prepared for some objections he might raise and could recognize that these were not a reflection on my capability as director but rather reflected shifting priorities in the organization. Because I could listen calmly instead of getting upset, I was able to take this new information and reformulate the rejected projects into acceptable ones.

If you too give yourself a chance and take time to use imagery creatively when you need a change in your life, you will find it a rewarding and relaxing activity. Have fun!

SECTION III :

TECHNIQUES THAT HELP YOU CHANGE YOUR LIFE AND REDUCE YOUR LOAD

11. LOOKING AT THE WORLD DIFFERENTLY

12. PUTTING YOURSELF IN SOMEONE ELSE'S SHOES

13. GIVING UP BEING RIGHT

14. LEARNING TO DEAL WITH CRITICISM

15. NEEDING LESS APPROVAL FROM OTHERS

16. MANAGING YOUR TIME WISELY

17. BEING NICE TO YOURSELF

11

Change Your LIfe And Reduce Your Load By...........

Looking At The World Differently

We all have our own ways of looking at things, our own beliefs about what is good or bad, or about what people should or shouldn't do. We have developed these views and beliefs over our lifetimes as a result of what we have been taught and what we have learned through our own experiences.

It's as if we are living our lives inside a box with only a single window, so the one view we have of the outside world is what we see through that window. If we could step outside the box and walk around to another spot, our outlook might be completely different.

We construct our windows — or frame of reference — partially by creating beliefs, values and rules that help us learn how to get along in the world. Unfortunately, most of us also hold some views and beliefs which result in our experiencing a lot more stress and unhappiness in our lives than we would like to have.

The main reason this happens is that our beliefs and rules restrict our choices for ways we can behave in certain situations. So, when someone says something that "makes you mad," you don't see that you have a choice about whether or not to be angry, because you believe that when someone speaks to you that way, you **have to** get mad.

CHANGING YOUR VIEW

Fortunately, we can change our views and beliefs so that we see the world differently. Let's look at an example of the way this can work.

> Joyce was very upset about one of her coworkers at the office. Everyone in the office is in and out during the day, and when they

are in the office they are supposed to share equally in answering the phones, dealing with walk-in clients, and generally taking charge of the office. The problem is that one woman, Lucille, never does her share. She just keeps on doing her paper work, leaving whoever else is in the office to handle everything. "I just can't stand to be in the office with her," says Joyce. "I try to work it out so that we're there at different times, but I can't always do that. She just makes me so mad! Whenever I'm there with her I get a terrific headache and it usually lasts the rest of the day."

We asked Joyce whether she had told Lucille how she felt. "Yes," she said, "but it doesn't do any good. Other people have told her too, but she doesn't care. She just does what she wants."

We asked Joyce whether she had tried any other ways to change Lucille. "I've tried everything I can think of," she said. "I've tried just letting the phone ring to see if she'll answer it, or telling her I'm busy so she'll have to handle the walk-ins. But nothing works. I'm fed up with her!"

We asked Joyce whether she wanted to continue to feel tense and upset and get headaches every time she is in the office with Lucille. "Of course I don't," said Joyce, "but I can't seem to find a way to make her change."

We asked Joyce what else could change in this situation that might possibly make things better. "Well I guess I could find another job," said Joyce, "but I like the job except for this one thing, and I really don't want to leave. I can't think of anything else that could change unless Lucille leaves, and I don't think she's about to do that."

We pointed out to Joyce that in fact it looked like she couldn't change Lucille, but that we could see another solution besides leaving her job. We suggested to Joyce that she could change her way of looking at the situation. That way she could change the way she felt about what was going on, and she would no longer have to be upset and get headaches when she was in the office with Lucille.

It wasn't Lucille who was **making** Joyce upset. **Joyce** was making Joyce upset. Joyce obviously believed that "everything has to be fair"; that "everyone should do their share." When someone acted in a way that didn't fit this belief, Joyce got upset. So it was Joyce's beliefs that were creating the stress, which **were** within her power to change.

We suggested to Joyce that because she had already tried everything she could think of to change the situation and it hadn't worked, she might begin working instead on changing her own reactions to the situation. We suggested that she should **choose** not to be upset about it. Instead, she should look at it as an **opportunity**

> to learn to deal with unfairness in life. We also suggested that she begin looking for good qualities in Lucille and even complimenting her when she gets the chance. For example, Lucille may have a nice laugh, or dress well. If Joyce found something to like in Lucille, she would gradually begin to find her easier to be with.
>
> Joyce decided to try this, by choosing not to **let** Lucille's behavior upset her, and by deciding not to complain to her friends anymore about Lucille because that only reinforced her anger. She began to look for and acknowledge good qualities in Lucille.
>
> Joyce reported back that while making this change took some effort and work, she and Lucille now have a more congenial relationship. They still aren't close and probably never will be, but Joyce feels they have reached a mutual understanding. Lucille's work habits haven't changed, but she is more friendly now.
>
> Joyce summed up her experiment this way: "I feel so much better about this situation because I dislike having unsettled and negative relationships in my life. Now I have learned that I can change a negative relationship and turn it into a better one."

You may find this a strange solution to Joyce's problem. After all, the situation was unfair to Joyce, wasn't it? Why should she just give in and take it, letting Lucille get away with that?

We would never recommend that a person just let someone walk all over them. If you **can** change an undesirable situation, you should do so. But often we find, as Joyce did, that we cannot change another person's behavior no matter how much we try. If you will examine your experience, you will find that it is very difficult to change another person. The easiest person for you to change is **you!** Even though you cannot change a situation you find upsetting, you **can choose** not to find it upsetting.

CHOOSING INSTEAD OF REACTING

Choosing to look at things differently is not easy. It means giving up some views and beliefs we have had for a long time. For example, Joyce had the view that "everything has to be fair." That's a great idea, and deep down most of us probably believe it. At the same time, we have learned in life that everything **isn't** always fair. So we have a choice. We can continue to believe that everything should be fair, and whenever something happens to us that doesn't seem fair, we can get very upset — maybe even sick. Or we can just decide that sometimes things are fair and sometimes they aren't, and that what is important to us is feeling good, so we're just not going to let the unfair things that happen to us upset us.

We may feel that we're letting other people take advantage of us — that we're getting "conned." But think about it. If you're doing what you're doing because you **choose** to do it, can someone be taking advantage of you? Of course not. You are in charge of your life, and **you** are choosing to feel good. You are choosing to look at life differently so that a situation that formerly upset you doesn't upset you any more.

LOOK AT YOUR OWN BELIEFS

To get a better picture of some beliefs that may be causing you stress, complete each of the following sentences with the first response that comes to mind:

I think it is very important for me to ....

It really makes me angry when someone ....

I am a person who always ....

I feel guilty if I don't ....

I worry about what other people will think when I ....

I usually get upset when ....

Life should be ....

Now think about one or two times recently when you felt very upset. Try to discover what beliefs or views you have about life that made those situations so distressing to you. For example, you may believe that everyone should like you and be nice to you all the time, or that when someone does something "bad" they should be punished. See if you can let go of your belief and rethink the situation as just something that is happening, but doesn't have to be upsetting. See if you can look at such situations as challenges and opportunities — not as misery.

LISTEN TO WHAT YOU SAY TO YOURSELF

Another way to change the way you feel about a situation is to pay attention to what you are telling yourself about what is going on. Write down what you are saying to yourself about a stressful situation. Include both the facts of what happened and your thoughts about these events. Then analyze your thoughts to see whether you can find other choices or alternative ways of seeing the situation.

As an example, consider the situation of Catherine mother of an unusually intelligent son, Jason. Jason was in gifted programs throughout grade school and high school, was an honor graduate and won academic scholarships to college. He started college in the honors program of a major university but dropped out after one semester to return home and go to the local college. After two semesters, he dropped out again to get a job and devote most of his time to playing in a band. Catherine and Jason got into many heated arguments about his decision.

Here's Catherine's analysis of what she was saying to herself and her suggestions for less stressful, alternate views:

Statements to Myself	**Alternate Views**
"He's stupid! He's ruining his life."	"He's certainly not stupid. I know he's always been bright. Maybe he's thought more about this than I think."
"He thinks jobs are just waiting for him without any training or skill. He thinks life is easy."	"He's had jobs and he knows they aren't easy to get. He also knows how to work hard."
"He doesn't care about anyone but himself."	"He really is worried about disappointing us, but he's just not interested in studying and he wants to get this band together."
"I really messed up somehow in bringing him up if he would do such a silly thing."	"I'm not responsible for his choices now that he's grown up. I did my best for him. Now he has to set his own goals."
"I need to find some way to make him see that he's making a big mistake."	"I can't control his life. He really needs my support to know that it's allright for him to establish his independence in his own way."

CHANGING UPSET INTO CHALLENGE

Hearing about the way someone else chose to turn an upsetting situation into a challenge that could be dealt with will make the use of this technique clearer to you. Here is an example where someone chose to look at a stressful situation differently and got results that surprised her.

Leslie: Giving Up Rescuing

I have always experienced a lot of stress with my mother. Somehow, I never have seemed to be able to do things in a way that pleases her. In this situation it was worse than usual because she was in the hospital, having had surgery, and complaining about everything. She was upset because she wasn't allowed to smoke, didn't like the food, didn't like being in a room with other people, felt that the nurses weren't sympathetic, etc. She kept crying and complaining and I kept trying to fix everything up and make her feel better. I jumped from rescue to rescue as she jumped from complaint to complaint. Of course, my attempts to solve Mother's problems and make things peaceful were a failure, and as usual I was soon as upset as she was. ...

As I was complaining to my husband that evening about the situation with mother, I suddenly remembered the ideas about choosing to look at things differently. I was finally able to hear what my husband had been telling me for a long time — that it is not possible for me to keep my mother happy all the time, and I am making myself miserable by trying. I realized that somehow I believed that I had to rescue Mother quickly and properly or else I would be a bad person deserving of her anger. ...

So the next day I decided to try an experiment. I would do what I reasonably could to make Mother comfortable. Then, if she was still upset and angry, I would let her be upset, and I would remind myself that her anxiety and anger are not really directed at me, but at herself and her circumstances. ...

At first it was very hard, but I sat there letting her be upset and feeling a little sick to my stomach. As the day wore on though, it was easier for me to accept her being upset without feeling I had to rescue her. It's amazing what a relief it was not to feel that I had to somehow solve every problem that came up. For the rest of the time she was in the hospital, and even now that she's home, I felt much less stress being with her — because I no longer believe I am completely responsible for keeping her happy.

Obviously, it was not Leslie's mother who was making Leslie upset in this situation. It was Leslie herself who was creating the stress by means of her belief that it was necessary for her to make her mother happy. When Leslie had that belief and at the same time was unable to make her mother happy, she felt extremely anxious and upset.

Fortunately, Leslie was able to realize that she could not solve her problem by changing her mother or the situation, but could solve it by changing her belief. By telling herself that it was okay for her mother to be upset and that she didn't have to feel responsible and anxious whenever that happened, Leslie was able to experience a previously stressful situation more comfortably. By looking at her world differently, Leslie changed her world!

12

Change Your Life And Reduce Your Load By...........

Putting Yourself In Someone Else's Shoes

When you find yourself involved in a situation with another person that is upsetting or stressful in some way, the chances are that you and this other person have different points of view about what happened. Furthermore, it is unlikely that you can — or even want to — understand the other person's viewpoint of what occurred. This is true because when you are intensely involved in a situation you tend to be blinded by your strong feelings about it. You see only your own perspective of what went on.

ADVANTAGES OF SEEING ANOTHER VIEW

You may be saying, "So what? Why should I want to see the other person's point of view when I'm upset. I have enough problems of my own!" Well, believe it or not, seeing the other person's perspective helps you be less emotionally involved in what is happening and therefore more able to see solutions to the problem. It gives you a way of emotionally stepping back and seeing the situation as if you were someone watching it instead of someone intensely involved in it. It allows you to be more objective and clearheaded about the way you deal with the other person, which means you have a better chance of resolving the situation and not feeling upset anymore.

We all have the ability to put ourselves in the other person's shoes but many people don't have much practice in actually doing it. The exercises in this chapter will give you some practice in taking the perspective of another person so that you will be able to use this technique to defuse tense situations in your life.

HOW TO PUT YOURSELF IN THE OTHER'S SHOES

Read the following description of an event:

> You are waiting to check out in the grocery store. Several people are in front of you in line. The line is moving very slowly. The clerk seems to be having some problems with the machine. Suddenly the man in front of you starts shouting at the clerk, "C'mon, hurry it up, honey! We haven't got all day to stand here while you mess around." The clerk looks up but doesn't say anything. The man complains disgustedly, "If these grocery stores didn't hire such stupid people they'd do a lot more business." When the clerk still ignores him, he dumps his groceries on the floor and stomps off, mumbling, "that's the last time I'll shop in this store."

Think about this event. Who did you see as the "bad guy"? Most people see the man who shouted as the "bad guy." **Now rewrite the episode from the point of view of this man.** To do this you should imagine you are the man and write down the thoughts and conscious experiences you have as this man during the occasion just described. In other words, try to experience the incident as the man did. Do this before reading any more of this page.

Now, look at what you have written. If you were really able to see the man's point of view, you might have written something like this:

> Boy, I've had a hard day. The boss was really in a foul mood. And now I have to stop at the store, just because my wife forgot milk and lettuce and didn't want to go out again. Why is this line moving so slowly? I have a lot of work to do tonight and it's late already. That clerk doesn't look like she knows what she's doing. And everybody else just stands here and takes it. Stores just don't care about customers like they used to. If we don't complain, nothing will ever change.

In other words, what you have just read could have been what the man was thinking and feeling.

On the other hand, if you were not putting yourself in the man's shoes, you may have written something like this:

> That man is a jerk. He just thinks everybody should jump whenever he wants something. He's probably very insecure and he shouts like that to make himself feel important. His parents probably spoiled him rotten when he was a kid and now he always wants his own way.

If you wrote things like this, you were not putting yourself in the man's shoes, because it is not very likely that he was thinking these things about himself in that situation. In this example, there are **three types of statements that show that whoever wrote it was not seeing things from the man's point of view:**

(1) Statements **evaluating** the man, like "he's a jerk." The man would not have been thinking this about himself.

(2) Statements **analyzing** the man, like "He's insecure." The man would not have been saying this to himself about himself.

(3) Statements **explaining** the man, like "His parents probably spoiled him." He would not have been thinking this.

If you **were** actually putting yourself in the man's shoes, as in the first example, you would have been writing statements that describe what is going on from his point of view, not attempting to evaluate him.

Now that you have put yourself in the man's shoes, how do you feel about him compared to how you felt before? Most people feel less negative toward someone after really seeing that person's point of view.

TAKING PERSPECTIVE IN YOUR OWN LIFE

Of course the example you just worked on was not a situation in which you were emotionally involved. We used it merely to demonstrate the technique. Now you are ready to try the method with a situation from your own life.

Choose a recent situation in which you were upset. It's best to begin with one in which you were not extremely upset (you can get to those later). Choose a situation you are still unhappy about; one that has not been resolved completely. First write a few sentences describing the situation — just explaining what happened. Now imagine you are the **other person** in this situation. Put yourself inside that person's head and write down what you imagine he or she was thinking, feeling, or experiencing during the incident. Take the perspective of the other person as completely as possible. Be sure not to evaluate, analyze, or explain the person, just describe his or her point of view. Include how the other person felt toward you.

Now ask yourself how you feel toward the other person. Do you understand this person better? Do you have any new ideas of ways you can approach this person and work to resolve the situation?

You will find that this technique works best if you actually **write**

down the other person's point of view, rather than just thinking about it. Most people find that they get a more complete picture and more effective results when they write out the other person's perspective.

Try this technique next time you find yourself stewing over a conflict. As the following examples show, most people find that it helps them feel more calm about the situation, as well as making the conflict easier to resolve.

HOW THIS TECHNIQUE WORKS FOR OTHERS

After trying this procedure a few times, people frequently find that although it is an effort they can perceive their conflicts with other people quite differently than they had before. Here are a few examples:

Carl: Attacked By An Angry Tenant

I manage a 64-unit apartment complex. Since I usually get along well with the tenants, I was surprised when a new tenant verbally attacked me not long ago. She began by saying in a cold voice that the apartment was not what she had been shown before (which made no sense as they are all identical), that it was poorly constructed, and that her husband was allergic to the carpet and the insulation. She made several other statements that seemed unreasonable and ended by saying, "And I have a lawyer."

I was tempted to reply, "So, I have a lawyer too, and your husband's allergies are not my problem. And if he's allergic to the carpet and insulation, why did you rent this in the first place? You saw these apartments before and were told they were all alike, so I don't know what your problem is, lady."

Instead, I tried to see the situation from her point of view. I thought that she looked tired and worried and might be thinking about how she really didn't like the apartment much because it is small and about how hard it is to ever find anything that satisfies her husband.

So, I told her that I was sorry the apartment wasn't what she had expected and if there were problems I'd have them fixed immediately. I also said that I imagined it was difficult to find a place with such an allergy problem.

She sighed and talked about how tough it was, and ended up apologizing for being so short.

Kay: A Stormy Teenage Shopping Session

My teenage son needed a new winter coat. In many trips to many stores we hadn't been able to find a coat he liked. Finally he found a style he liked in a local store, but they didn't have his size.

(He's not quite big enough for a man's small size.) A week later the store called me to say they had a small and a medium women's size in a unisex color.

I felt excited at the prospect of getting a coat he really liked and of ending the frustrating search. But when I took him down there, it turned out that both coats were too small. He got angry with me for having told him that his coat was in when actually the ones that had come in were in women's sizes. I got mad. We went home furious with each other.

In my angry thoughts I was evaluating him by thinking things like, "He must enjoy driving me crazy. If he weren't so picky he would have found a coat long ago." I was also analyzing him with thoughts like, "Maybe he's just needing more attention from me and the only way he can get it is in shopping time."

Then I decided to try writing down what might be his perspective. This is what I wrote: "I can't stand it when she sets me up like this. She's so gushy to sales people, it makes me feel like a jerk. She's so anxious to be nice to them she doesn't care about me. I'll never find a decent coat. I'll never get big enough for regular men's sizes. It's hopeless."

After this attempt to stand in my son's place and feel what he might be feeling, I was able to talk calmly to him and tell him I realized he was older now and could be responsible for choosing his own wardrobe. I told him I realized how important it is for him to find the right coat and that we would keep looking. He thanked me and told me he would try not to take so long making up his mind when we shop for his clothes in the future.

Ted: Friendly Family Arguments

In my family, when we were growing up we had long discussions — or you might call them arguments — over just about everything. And to this day it's really no different. When my brothers and I are together with my parents we can get going on just about any topic. Sometimes this is friendly, but a lot of times it leads to hard feelings too.

I'll have to admit I'd never thought much about seeing their point of view. In fact, one time about a month ago my brother and my mother and I were arguing about politics for about an hour, and it wasn't until my mother pointed out that we were all on the same side that I realized it myself. By that time I had gotten myself pretty worked up — and all for no reason except that I was too caught up in the situation to realize that there really wasn't any argument.

Anyway, for the last few weeks, since I did those exercises on seeing the other person's point of view, I have been trying this with my family. I have found that I am much like a child in that I have a lot of difficulty taking another perspective into account. And I think this leads me to a lot of anxiety, anger, and hostility. The way I am working on this problem is by making a conscious effort to listen to other people's viewpoints, writing down later what I think they were saying, thinking, and feeling.

So many times in the past I have gotten involved in arguments and gotten mad, where if I had only taken the time to really listen to what the other person was saying, I could have avoided the argument. Now I try to repeat silently to myself that my point of view isn't the only way to look at the situation.

Marie: The Partying Husband

I found the exercises on seeing the other person's point of view simply fantastic! I think this will be something I can use over and over again. The first time I had a lot of trouble with it. I took one issue that, although it was over with and supposedly settled, I had never really accepted. It was very difficult for me to see things from this person's perspective, but I couldn't give up on it. I finally finished it and felt a lot better about the whole episode.

I have since used this technique in a couple of other situations and found it very helpful in both instances. I'll describe one of them for you. One evening I was getting worried because my husband was late getting home from work. I finally heard from him about ten o'clock. He called from a friend's house and invited me to come over. When I got there I found that they had all been drinking for a few hours before I got there. My husband had had a very bad day at work and he was complaining to his friend about this. My husband got pretty drunk, and when he accidentally knocked something over, I got disgusted, screamed at him, and left.

All the way home I was fuming. I was furious with all of them for letting me worry so long and I felt embarrassed by the whole situation. I couldn't see my husband's point of view or sympathize with him at all. But after I got home I realized that I was only making the whole situation worse by reacting in a stubborn and childish way. I was able to sit down and write out the whole situation from his point of view. I felt much calmer by the time he got home and wasn't angry any more. This made it easier for us to talk about the whole thing the next day and work things out instead of being mad and not speaking to each other all day.

Karla: Sharing a Free Lunch

Since my friend Laura and I have both been out of work, neither of us has had much money for food lately. Laura kept coming over to eat with me, so I let her for a while, even though I hardly had any money for my own food and had been eating some at my mother's house.

I like Laura and I knew she was having a hard time. I wanted to help her, but at the same time I was feeling frustrated. I suggested she go to "We Serve" (a "soup kitchen"), but she refused. She wasn't able to say why she wouldn't go. I didn't want to keep on feeding her, but I also felt that since I did have some food I should continue.

Then I decided to see it from her point of view. I knew it wasn't Laura's "fault" that she didn't have money for food. I also knew she didn't like eating at my house so often but probably felt she had no choice.

When I was not taking Laura's perspective, I was getting more and more annoyed at her not going somewhere where I knew they could help her out. When I tried seeing her point of view, I changed the way I saw her refusal to go to "We Serve."

Instead of evaluating or analyzing her, I thought about how I would feel in her situation. When I did this, I realized that I **was** in her situation except that I had my mother's house to go to. I also thought she might feel too proud or too shy to go.

I thought that if it were me, it would help a lot if someone went with me the first time. I asked Laura if that would help her and she said "Yes." We have continued to go together some of the time and she is going most days now.

If I had not tried to see her point of view, I probably would have kept feeling increasingly more frustrated. Most likely I wouldn't have wanted her to come over to see me as often. Now instead of losing our friendship, we are actually better friends.

13

Change Your Life And Reduce Your Load By...........

Giving Up Being Right

While you've been reading the sections on looking at the world differently and putting yourself in someone else's shoes, you may have found yourself resisting the ideas presented. You might have been saying to yourself: "Look, I know I'm right in this situation. Why should I try to see someone else's point of view when I know I'm right?"

Before we answer that question, we'd like to tell you a story about a clever dog.

WHAT CAN WE LEARN FROM A DOG?

> Spot was an independent dog. He didn't have a master but he got along pretty well on his own. Every night at ten o'clock he went down to the back door of a certain restaurant in town where he always found some good steak bones and leftovers. Then, one night Spot showed up at the restaurant and there was nothing outside to eat. Spot ran all around the restaurant to make sure he was in the right place. He was. He barked a little to see if anyone would bring out the goodies. They didn't. He waited around for an hour or so, but nothing happened. He finally gave up and went home.
>
> The next night he went back and the same thing happened. Again, he left hungry. And the night after that was the same. Spot went to the right place at the right time but he didn't get any food.
>
> The following night was different. After he went back and the same thing happened, Spot decided to forget the restaurant he had been going to all this time, and try someplace else. Only a few blocks away he found an even better place with plenty of good bones, and he went home that night feeling happier and more satisfied than ever.

Now what was so smart about Spot? Well, believe it or not, Spot was a lot cleverer than many people often are. Spot was able to forget about being right and just do something that worked. Animals don't care about being right, they just want to feel good. People, strangely enough, often prefer to be right even when this makes them feel bad.

Spot knew he was in the right place at the right time, but when that wasn't working out for him any more he gave it up and went somewhere else. **People** would probably complain to their friends and get them to agree that this was a rotten deal. Then maybe they'd organize a group to wait out there every night until the food showed up. But all the time they were being right they'd be hungry.

LOSING WHEN YOU THINK YOU'RE WINNING

Now you may think people aren't this silly. Why would someone give up having what they really want just to be right about something? Well, let's look at some examples:

> Nick likes to go to parties with his girlfriend, Karen, and have a good time. "The only problem is," Nick complains, "that hardly ever happens anymore." What usually does happen is that when Nick is all set to leave for the party, Karen isn't ready yet. He waits around for a while and then starts getting impatient and yelling at Karen that he's sick and tired of sitting there cooling his heels while she messes around changing her clothes three times and deciding what to wear. She screams at him to get off her back and she'll be ready when she's ready. "So," Nick explains, "by the time we do finally leave, we're both in a rotten mood and that really spoils the evening for me."

> Margaret wants to get along with her teenaged daughter, Lisa. "We used to be such good friends and enjoyed doing things together," Margaret remembers, "but lately we fight all the time." The fights usually begin with Margaret pointing out to Lisa that her room is a terrible mess and that she should spend less time on the phone and more time cleaning things up. Then Lisa reminds her mother that it's **her** room and she'll clean it up when **she** wants to. Margaret starts yelling at Lisa that her whole problem is that she just isn't responsible about getting things done and that if she wants to be treated like an adult she's going to have to start acting like one. Lisa yells back that just because her mother never has any fun she doesn't want anybody else to have any either. "Anyway," Margaret sighs, "we never have any fun together anymore and I miss that."

As you were reading these examples, you were probably trying to decide who was right and who was wrong. Who you selected as the "right" one in these incidents very likely depends on your point of view. For example, if you are the parent of a teenager, you probably felt Margaret is right in the second example — that it is Lisa's fault they aren't getting along. On the other hand, if you are a teenager, or a young adult who remembers such conflicts with your parents, you probably feel that Lisa is right — that it's Margaret who is causing all the problems.

The point we would like to make here is that it's irrelevant who is right. What is important is that the way these people are behaving is not working for them. They aren't getting what they want. They aren't enjoying life, or enjoying being with a person they love! Then why do they keep doing it? Because they **know** they're right, and they don't want to give in.

Let's just look at the people who told the stories here; they were the ones who were specifically complaining that they weren't getting what they wanted. Nick wants to go to parties with Karen and have a good time, but he isn't getting that. Margaret wants to have fun with her daughter and get along well with her but isn't.

They each believe that they're right, and if the other person would change — Karen become more conscious of time, Lisa become more responsible — then they would get what they want. The problem is that this isn't happening. Margaret and Nick are continuing to stick to their behavior — because they know they're right — even though they aren't getting what they want by doing this.

LETTING GO

Unfortunately, Margaret and Nick aren't behaving as intelligently as Spot was. When Spot didn't get what he wanted, he changed his behavior so he could get it. He didn't care about being right.

Margaret and Nick could do this too. Probably, if Nick tried some other ways of dealing with Karen's lateness — like watching a television show while he waited, or going on to the party and having her meet him there, or waiting until she was almost ready before he arrived — he would find a new way to deal with the situation so that they could leave for the party feeling happy with themselves and each other.

Similarly, Margaret could consider alternative ways of dealing with her feelings about Lisa's room — like ignoring it, or cleaning it herself, or offering to help Lisa clean it. Eventually, she would probably find a way that worked so that she and Lisa could stop fighting over this issue.

This way of dealing with problems that cause stress in your life may seem strange to you. Certainly it isn't easy. We are all well-trained in being right. Somehow, anything else seems like giving in, like being taken advantage of. What we forget is that as long as we're not getting what we want, there really isn't much satisfaction in being right. In fact, by insisting on repeating this "right" behavior that doesn't work we are making **ourselves** miserable.

USING THIS TECHNIQUE IN YOUR LIFE

Take a look at your life. Think of someone you continually have conflicts with. Now think of one specific type of situation where this conflict occurs between the two of you. What usually happens? What do each of you say and do? Now ask yourself three questions:

- Are you the one who is right in these situations?
- Is your behavior getting you what you want in these instances?
- Would you rather be right or get what you want?

Be honest with yourself. If you decide you'd rather get what you want, think of some new ways you can behave in this situation the next time it comes up. If you find yourself reluctant to try these new ways, ask yourself if that is because the next behavior involves giving up being right.

Here are two examples in which people found that they could defuse tense situations by giving up their insistence on being right:

Carla: I Just Want To Go To The Party

Last week an old childhood friend of mine invited me to a party. I really wanted to go because a lot of my old friends would be there. I knew my boyfriend, Doug, wouldn't want to go to this party, because he never wants to go to parties with these friends. (Once he did go and was so uncomfortable he left after half an hour.) I also knew he wouldn't want me to go by myself, and that if I insisted on it, we would probably have a big fight.

Usually, when situations like this had arisen in the past, I either didn't go to the party, or I told Doug I was going even if he didn't want to — and then we'd have a fight. He would say things like, "You care more about those dumb friends than you do about me"; and "I'm tired of playing second fiddle to your friends, so if you go to that party you'd better look for a new boyfriend while you're there." I would get really mad because it seemed that Doug was thinking only of himself and the sacrifice he'd have to make by going with me or agreeing to my going alone. I always tried to show him how he was wrong for not thinking of me as an adult who has the right to go where I want to go when I want to go there. None of this ever got me what I really wanted — which was to go to the party and not have a fight with Doug. ...

This time I was determined to go and determined to do so without a fight. So I decided to try letting Doug be right and not argue with him. I decided not to try to convince him I was right in wanting to go to the party or that he was wrong to get mad at me for going. I just told him about the party, that I was going, and that he was also invited and I'd like to have him come. He got mad as usual and started shouting, but I just said "You're right, sometimes I do put my friends and myself first, and I can see why you get mad when I do that."

It was easy not to get mad at him as long as I kept reminding myself that my goal was not to convince Doug he was wrong but just to go to the party. When I didn't fight back, Doug calmed down and we were actually able to have a calm discussion about the whole situation. He explained that he was insecure about our relationship because of my sexual activity before we met. I was able to reassure him about how much I care for him while also conveying to him how much it meant to me to go to this party.

Anyway, it all ended up that I did go to the party alone and Doug wasn't nearly as upset afterwards as he usually is. Doug feels better about our relationship and I think we've found some better ways of dealing with our conflicts.

Virginia: We All Forget Sometimes

It was Saturday afternoon. Looming up from the bottom of the garage steps was a large brown trash can. Anyone planning on walking into the house would either have to wedge past my car and the trash can to get up the steps or be extremely daring and leap over the can like an Olympic hurdler. Each day for the past three days, I had asked my seventeen-year-old son, Kevin, to put the trash can back in the corner of the garage where it belongs. He said he would, but he didn't do it.

It seems that when he first brought the trash can back up the driveway on Wednesday, trash day, one of the garage doors was shut. It was hard to maneuver the can around the cars, so rather than take the time to open the west garage door, he left the can at the foot of the stairs. I asked him that night to put it away correctly. He said okay. The next day as he was leaving to go out with a friend, I told him again to put the can away before he left. He said that he forgot and would do it immediately. But here it was Saturday and the can was still there.

I was irritated. It seemed as is he seldom remembered to follow through on the most basic maintenance aspects of life. Bringing up dirty dishes and clothes, locking the front door at night, letting the dog outside, carrying his driver's license with him, keeping track of his car keys-- all seemed to fall into the trash bin of his memory. ...

When he came home that Saturday afternoon from an out- of-town debate clinic, I told him he was grounded that night. Kevin said okay but he thought it was dumb and too severe to ground him over a "stupid trash can." I told him I didn't care what he thought. He had not followed through on the task. His voice started rising and he began lecturing me loudly about my lack of perspective on the situation. ...

Now this kid is a championship debater who thinks that life is one big debate contest. He thinks that the louder and more aggressive his voice, the better his chance of winning an argument. I told him that I didn't want to debate him. He was to take his punishment and be quiet. I was beginning to get hot under the collar. He continued to give me his opinion and I told him I was tired of his debating me every time he was disciplined. I don't mind honest discussion when there is a disagreement, but as his mother, I will establish the rules. I finally told him to "shut up!" ...

As he walked away, he said that if he didn't know when to shut up, it was because he got it from me. I was furious! Who did this kid think he was talking to anyway? As a high school counselor, listening is probably one of my strongest skills. In my opinion, I thought he was a lucky kid to have a mother who was such a good listener and so patient with his daily irresponsibility. I was doing him a favor by trying to teach him to follow through on tasks carefully.

I shook my finger at him and told him he was never to talk to me that way again. As long as he lived in my house he would be respectful when he talked with me. He stood there and looked at me for a moment and then turned around and walked away. He had enough sense not to carry the issue any further. He stayed home that night and hung around in his room working on a debate case. ....

I began to think about how easy it is for Kevin and me to slip into battles with each other. I felt sad that it had happened again when what I really want is for us to laugh and play more together. I know he feels that sometimes I treat him like a child, even though he actually is responsible in areas of his life that truly matter to him such as debate, school work and his job. He may view a displaced garbage can as trivial. Like most teenagers, he is less concerned with mundane custodial tasks in life than with social and academic issues. Also, he had a cold and was probably tired from the debate, so it probably wasn't an opportune time for me to jump him about the garbage can.

For several days, neither of us mentioned anything about our argument. The next Wednesday morning I had left a book at home, so I called Kevin and asked him to bring it with him to school. That night I remembered that I had an appointment the next morning to take my car in for repair, so I'd need to have him pick me up at the garage and give me a ride to school. He'd have to leave for school earlier than usual. I apologized for not telling him sooner. I'd known for a week and just forgotten to tell him.

He told me that it was okay because we are all human and we forget things sometimes. "Just remember," he said, "when you forget your book or you don't tell me about an appointment, that is just like the garbage can. I want you to understand that I forget sometimes too."

I bit my tongue and avoided pointing out to him the difference between occasional and daily forgetting. I let him make his point and I kept quiet — just smiled, told him he was absolutely correct, and walked upstairs. It felt better not to respond in anger. He was right. We all need a little breathing room sometimes just to be human and make mistakes. We were both winners this time.

Remember that, like Carla and Virginia, what you are looking for is a way of having less stress and more joy in your life. Insisting on being right generally adds to your stress because for you to be right you have to make someone else wrong. This leads to conflict, anxiety, and tension.

If your relationship with someone isn't working the way you want it to, ask yourself whether you want that relationship to work or whether you want to be right. When you get into a conflict with that person, ask yourself whether you will win by proving the other person wrong or by finding a way to be happy together. Then let yourself win. Be happy!

14

Change Your Life And Reduce Your Load By...........

Learning To Deal With Criticism

Most of us have at least some difficulty dealing with criticism. We all want to be liked and respected by others and we like to feel that others approve of our behavior. When someone specifically tells us that they don't like something we've said or done, we may feel inadequate, stupid, hurt, guilty, resentful, or angry. On the other hand, we **could** view the criticism simply as information and see this as an opportunity to find out something useful about the way another person reacts to our behavior.

HEARING CRITICISM AS INFORMATION

The big barrier that deters us from using the information we get from someone who criticizes us is our **feelings** about what it implies. Much of the time we are so blinded by our feelings that we can't really hear the information at all. Let's look at an example of the problems this creates.

> Jean feels terrible whenever her boss says something critical about her work. "Like the other day," says Jean, "when I showed him a report I'd worked really hard on. He said one section was too short and another section too long. I felt really dumb, like I always mess up everything. I thought to myself that my boss never has really liked me; he's always trying to remind me that he knows more than I do."

Jean is having trouble separating the way her boss feels about **her** and about **her work in general** from the way he feels about this **report.**

If she had responded only to the **information** the boss gave her, she could have said to herself, "Oh, this section needs to be longer and that one needs to be shorter. I can probably change that in a few hours." She could have saved herself the misery she felt from generalizing the critical comments. Once she generalizes the comments, she winds up feeling that the boss doesn't like her or any of her work. But her boss didn't **say** any of that! Jean herself came up with that, and even worse, she didn't check it out with her boss to find out if he felt that way. She just assumed he did.

It may surprise you to know that Jean is not unusual in the way she reacted to criticism. Many people — even those who appear to be highly successful and confident — are sensitive to critical comments. We ourselves find that when we are reading over the written evaluations participants give us at the end of one of our workshops we often give more weight to one negative remark than to twenty-five positive comments. Furthermore, we tend to remember those negative observations longer.

THE POWERFUL EFFECTS OF CRITICISM

Why do people react this way to criticism? Why does it have such a powerful effect on us? One reason is that most of us are not nearly so sure of ourselves and self-confident as we seem to be. Criticism brings up all those old negative feelings and self-doubts we have been trying to keep hidden. We react by feeling inadequate — as if some of those negative feelings about ourselves are really true. Or we may feel hurt or angry at the other person for reminding us of our inadequacies. Frequently, we feel guilty because we believe that we shouldn't make mistakes and that the criticism is evidence that we have done something "wrong." In any case, reacting in these ways to criticism adds stress and unhappiness to our lives.

It is possible to learn to react differently to criticism. To do this, you need to be aware of how you generally react to criticism now. If you answer the questions below as honestly as you can, you will learn something about yourself and how you deal with criticism.

HOW DO YOU DEAL WITH CRITICISM?

1. **When someone criticizes you, how do you usually reply?**
   ___Do you apologize?
   ___Do you defend yourself with excuses?
   ___Do you say something critical back to them?
   ___Do you tell them how hurt you feel?
   ___Do you ask them to explain what they mean and what changes they would like to see?

2. **When someone criticizes you, how do you usually feel?**
   ___Do you feel inadequate?
   ___Do you feel stupid?
   ___Do you feel resentful and angry?
   ___Do you feel hurt?
   ___Do you feel glad to get an honest opinion?
   ___Do you feel willing to ignore the comment if you decide it is not accurate?
   ___Do you feel interested in having the person explain further?

3. **What do you do with criticism when you get it?**
   ___Do you think about it for days afterward, feeling terrible about yourself?
   ___Do you feel angry and avoid the person who criticized you as much as possible.
   ___Do you consider honestly what was said, and ask yourself whether you want to make any changes?

If you selected any of the first four alternatives under either item 1 or 2, or the first two alternatives under item 3, you are reacting to criticism with negative thoughts and emotions that are upsetting you. Remember that it is these thoughts and feelings — **your own reactions** — that are making you upset. The critical comments by themselves have no power to disturb you.

If you're like most of us, you'll find you want to deal with criticism less stressfully and more usefully. You want to be able to respond to criticism without denying what was said, getting defensive, or attacking the other person. You want to be able to hear a critical comment as just what it is — one person's opinion.

You want to be able to hear what the person has to say and respond in a way that doesn't cause problems between you. Then you want to be able to consider the criticism objectively and decide whether you want to make any changes. Finally, you want to be able to take whatever action you have decided to take and then forget about the criticism altogether.

CHANGING YOUR FEELINGS ABOUT CRITICISM

Here is a short exercise that will help you start changing your feelings about criticism. You'll need paper and pencil.

1. **Think of someone who has criticized you.** Think of a situation in which that person criticized you. Write down what he or she said. Write down what you said back. Write down how you felt.

2. **Now imagine you are the other person.** Imagine yourself saying those critical words. How are you feeling as you say these words? Write that down. What are your motives? Write them down. What are you trying to communicate as you are making the critical comments? Write this down. How do you hope the person you are criticizing feels? Write this down.

3. **Now be yourself again.** Read what you wrote at the beginning about how you felt when you were criticized. Compare this to what you wrote when you imagined yourself as the other person. Do you think you got the message the other person wanted you to get? Or did you add some extra stuff and create your own message?

4. **What do you think now about the way you answered the person who criticized you?** Did your answer help you get as much information as possible from this person without annoying him or her? Can you think of a more useful way you could have replied?

This exercise is designed to help you decide whether your way of dealing with criticism works well for you. We're not saying there's a right or wrong way to deal with criticism. What we are saying is that some ways are less stressful and more useful than others.

Remember what we talked about in the chapter on giving up being right — it's what works that counts! Even if you are sure that someone is only criticizing you to manipulate you and give you a hard time, you are still better off not getting upset about it. If you argue and defend yourself, you will only spur the critic on to attack you even more. But, if you can hear what the person says, consider it objectively without getting upset, and decide what you want to do, criticism doesn't have to be a problem for you no matter what the other person's motives are.

DEALING WITH CRITICISM IN YOUR OWN LIFE

Try this procedure the next time someone criticizes you:

1. **Tell the person you want to be sure you understand what he or she said.** Then try repeating back to the person what you think he or she said. Remember not to deny the criticism, defend yourself, or attack the other person. Just concentrate on making sure you understand the message. For example, Jean might say, "let me be sure I've got this straight; you want this section longer and this one shorter. Right?"

2. **Ask the person to explain a little more about what he or she meant.** For example, Jean might ask, "I'm not sure I understand why you think the report would be better that way. Could you explain a little more?"

3. **After the person has explained his or her point of view, check out your understanding by repeating back what he or she said.** For example, Jean might say, " I see. You think the report will be easier for people to understand if it's set up that way. Right?"

4. **Now you are clear about what the other person is trying to communicate.** Depending on the situation, you may want to explain your point of view. In a case where you are simply justifying yourself— like, "I only did it this way because last time I did it you didn't like what I did either" — you will be better off not saying anything. But, if you feel you honestly have some important information to convey, go ahead. For example, Jean might say, "We've collected a lot of data for this long section, but the data for the short section are sparse, so if we want to change the report, we'll have to spend a couple of weeks collecting more data."

5. **Thank the person for his or her comments.**

6. **Decide how you will use the criticism.** In a case like Jean's, where her boss is commenting on a specific piece of work, she obviously has to resolve the situation with him. So after they have each explained their views, she will probably want to give her suggestions about how to handle the situation, find out what her boss thinks, and be sure they have agreed on a solution. When a friend or relative is commenting on your behavior, you may want to think about what they said before you decide what you will do. You may or may not want to discuss this further with the person and tell them what you have decided.

7. **Make sure the person who criticized you knows you appreciate his or her interest.**

8. **Make sure you know that the criticism is only one person's opinion of one aspect of your behavior.** You do not have to see it as representing anything more than that. The choice is yours.

This method of dealing with criticism is easy to remember as long as you keep in mind that you are simply making sure of two things:

1) That you got the message straight;

2) That the other person knows you appreciate his or her interest in you.

To do these two things, you must ask for as much information as you need to understand what the critic is telling you and you must check out your understanding with the critic. Then, you must find something to appreciate in the criticism and tell the critic what you appreciate. This may seem difficult at first, but you will find that if you look carefully you can always find **some** aspect of the situation to appreciate, even if it is only: "I know we haven't been getting along lately, and I appreciate your taking the time to let me know what I do that annoys you"; or even, "I appreciate your telling me that, because it gives me a chance to practice not getting so upset what someone criticizes me."

A CRITICAL EXAMPLE

Now, let's look at an example of someone using this technique of dealing with criticism. In this example, Janet is using her new skills to cope with criticism from her husband, Greg. The situation is one which has led to fights in the past — namely, Janet's choosing to go with some friends to a concert that Greg isn't interested in attending.

Greg: "I don't see why you always want to go to these concerts without me. Sometimes I think you're just looking for excuses to get away from me."

Janet: "I'm not sure I understand. Are you saying that you think I'm going to this concert to get away from you?"

Greg: "Well, it seems like you never want to do things I like to do."

Janet: "I don't really understand why you feel that way. Could you tell me specifically what you've suggested that I haven't wanted to do?"

Greg: "Well, last weekend I wanted to go bowling but you said that you were too busy."

Janet: "Oh, I see. You think because I can find the time to do things I like to do, but not to do things you like to do, that I really don't want to be with you. Is that it?"

Greg: "Well, that's how it feels sometimes."

Janet: "Well I'm really glad you told me that. I really hadn't thought of it that way. I was just thinking about how much I like this music, and that I'm looking forward to hearing the concert. Actually, I would like to do something together this weekend. How about going out for dinner and a movie tomorrow night?"

Notice that Janet did not reply to Greg's criticism by denying the truth of his accusations, by making excuses, or by pointing out all Greg's bad points. All she did was make sure she got his message straight and let him know she appreciated his letting her know how he felt. Then she decided how she wanted to deal with Greg's comments and suggested a solution to him.

You may feel that Janet should have stood up for herself and argued with Greg. Similarly, you may feel that if you use this technique we have suggested for dealing with criticism, you will be letting people take advantage of you. But remember, what Janet wanted was to avoid a fight with her husband, and not to have hard feelings between them. By really hearing what Greg said, and responding to it, she achieved her purpose. Notice, also, that she did not give up going to the concert or agree that she was a bad person because she chose to go.

When you use this technique, keep in mind that your purpose is to avoid the stress of conflict with that person, or of feeling that you are wrong, stupid, or a bad person. By responding only to the **information** in the criticism, and not to all the implications you think it may have, you can avoid this stress. What you then decide to do with the criticism is another matter. You're always free to say something like, "I understand that you think I'm lazy when I sleep late on weekends and I still plan to sleep late." That is, you can **hear** the criticism without feeling upset, and without deciding to change. You don't have to let criticism be a source of stress for you!

REMEMBERING THE GOAL

After learning about these techniques for dealing with criticism, Thomas tried them out on his father and reported back on the following incident:

My father has always been pushy and critical. He may think he's "doing it for my own good," but I've always found his fault-finding remarks extremely irritating. Even now that I'm 35 years old, he still treats me like a kid — and when he does it I feel like a kid and act like a kid. But, since he lives 400 miles away and I don't see him very often, I'd really like to have our visits together be more pleasant. I've been wanting to find some new ways to respond to his criticism so that we don't get into so many fights.

When my wife Connie and I went back there last week for Thanksgiving, I decided to try this new approach. Our entire family was gathering for the weekend. Dad is a minister and he enjoys having Connie and me play our trumpets in church, so he had asked us to play that Sunday morning. He had arranged an accompanist for us and had told me to call her as soon as we got in to arrange a practice time. ...

We didn't get there until after 4:00. I didn't call the accompanist right away. There was something else I wanted to do first. It has become a tradition that when my brother, brother-in-law and I get together, we play basketball. For me this is a very enjoyable from of interaction between us and something I really look forward to. Since the sun was going down and we didn't have much time to play, we got out on the court. ...

Pretty soon my father drove up and we stopped playing to let him drive into the garage. He got out, and immediately asked me, "Have you called Maxine (the accompanist) yet?" I responded, "No, I haven't." Right away he started in: "I thought I told you to call her right away when you got here. Why can't I ever count on you to remember anything? You always seem to think you can let things go until you're good and ready no matter what other people's plans are."

I felt like telling him to forget the whole thing, but instead, I said, "I appreciate your arranging things with Maxine and I will call her when the sun goes down in about 15 minutes and it's too dark to play. I know she needs to have the practice time scheduled this evening." My father mumbled something like, "Okay, but be sure you don't forget," and walked on into the house. We played for a few more minutes and then I went in and called Maxine. ...

I felt good because I had handled the situation in what seemed like an adult way instead of blowing up like I usually do. In the past when my father made this type of remarks, we had always gotten into an argument that ruined the whole evening. This time nothing more was said about it and we went on to have a pleasant weekend.

15

Change Your Life And Reduce Your Load By...........

Needing Less Approval From Others

We've spent some time talking about reactions to criticism and how these responses can be stressful. Underlying the difficulties in dealing with criticism is another source of stress — **need for approval.** We're not just talking about wanting to have friends and please them, or about wanting to do a really good job on a new assignment. We're talking about **needing** approval from virtually everyone almost all the time. For example, consider the case of Pete:

> When Pete was growing up his father always told him, "Working hard and going that extra mile is the way to be a winner." His father was a very successful businessman and Pete wanted to be just as successful, so he has always tried to follow this advice. Pete was also an athlete in school and remembers how his coaches made him work to keep in shape and told him how important it is to stay in shape all your life. Pete agrees with this and he finds time to exercise on a regular basis.
>
> Pete also remembers that when he was growing up his father wasn't around much. He recalls his mother telling him many times that she hoped he would be a "real" husband and father when he got married. Now that Pete is married and has children he makes sure that he does his share around the house and has time to spend with his family.
>
> This might all be fine, except that Pete's boss is a very demanding man. He expects Pete to work on evenings and weekends frequently and also be involved in community service to uphold the image of the company. He also insists that Pete and his wife be involved in entertaining prospective clients for the company, often on very short notice.

Pete obviously doesn't have the time or the energy to do all this. He is under a lot of stress right now because he doesn't feel comfortable not doing any of the things he should do, or refusing any requests to do even more. At the same time, he doesn't feel good about himself because he doesn't feel that he is doing a really first-rate job at anything.

TWO WAYS OF TRYING TOO HARD

Pete actually has two problems related to needing approval that are causing him stress. First, he is trying to please too many people — that's why he can't say no to requests. Second, he expects too much from himself — he is trying to be the person he thinks everyone wants him to be. Pete cannot possibly live up to all these expectations or do all that is asked of him, but he thinks he somehow **should** do it all. Consequently, he feels like a failure. He looks at other people who he thinks are managing better and he asks himself, "Why can't I run my life like they do?"

Pete could eliminate a lot of stress from his life, as we all can, by keeping in mind two important principles;

1) You can't and don't need to get approval from everyone all the time.

2) Sometimes when you think you are trying to get others' approval it is actually yourself you are trying to please.

PLEASING OTHER PEOPLE

Let's talk about these ideas in more detail. First, let's look at the problems of trying to get approval from others all the time. Psychologists have talked for a long time about the difficulties inherent in measuring your self-worth by the amount of approval you get from others. Since it is **impossible** to please **everyone all** the time, if you try to do this, you are doomed to failure. Failure creates stress and it's also not good for your self-esteem.

Moreover, it is very difficult to assertively tell people what **you** want if you are always looking for approval. You won't want to send back an unsatisfactory meal in a restaurant because you'll be afraid the waiter will be angry. You'll be so concerned about losing the good will of others that you'll either end up doing things you don't want to do with people you don't want to do them with (and feeling imposed upon), or telling "social lies" to get out of it (and feeling guilty).

All this, just because you think the other person may dislike you if you tell the truth. This can also be a problem on the job. You may take on so many extra assignments because of fear of refusing a request that you are under constant pressure from work overload.

PLEASING YOURSELF

Sometimes, as Frances discovered, we tell ourselves we are trying to meet the expectations of others when it is actually **our own** approval we are after. She said:

> I like to give people praise and compliments when they do something good. I, in turn, enjoy receiving praise for the good things I do. Also, at times I am timid and apprehensive to tell people what **I** want because I do not want disapproval from them or to cause any hard feelings. Although this may be a very simplistic view, I like to see people happy and have everything agreeable. I am very sensitive and sympathetic to what other people are feeling, so I try not to cause any problems and try to make things easier for others.
>
> I am learning that it is very difficult to be assertive and tell people how I feel with an attitude like this. I feel burdened by always thinking how the other person will feel if I say what I want to say. I have realized that it is my own needs I am trying to fulfill. I am working on feeling ok about myself and realizing that if people do not like or agree with what I have to say, that's ok too.

Pete also had fallen into this trap. He had taken what he learned when he was growing up and made this into his image of what a good person should do — work hard long hours, keep fit, spend lots of time with his family, succeed in business, etc. There is nothing wrong with any of these behaviors. The problem for Pete was that he couldn't possibly do all that. He knew he was under stress, but he thought it was because other people expected so much of him. It was quite a surprise for Pete to realize that **he** was the one who expected all this from himself.

WHO ARE YOU TRYING TO PLEASE?

Take a look at your images of yourself. Are you:

- *Always the responsible one who takes care of arrangements and details?*
- *Always the life of the party?*
- *Always the perfect housekeeper?*
- *Always the easy-going accommodating one?*
- *Always the one who is available when someone has a problem?*

Obviously, these are all fine traits, but the can also be very confining. The problem is the **always**. When we see ourselves in one of these ways, it is easy to slip into feeling that other people expect it of us and to feel burdened by these expectations. In fact others are often more willing to give us a break than we are.

Actually, other people probably don't want you to be perfect. If you don't believe this, ask yourself how you feel about people you see as perfect in some way. For example, how do you feel visiting the perfect housekeeper? Do you feel comfortable discussing your marriage problems with someone who has a perfect marriage? Research shows that people see mistakes as humanizing and will generally like you better if you don't seem perfect.

What are your expectations of yourself? Say to yourself:

"I am a person who always ...."

Complete that sentence for yourself as many times as you can. Do you realize that these are **your** expectations of yourself? Do you believe that others expect you to be perfect? Can you give yourself a break from these expectations at times? Imagine that you have **chosen** not to do what you **always** do. How do you feel? Free? Guilty? Relaxed? Worried?

GIVE YOURSELF A BREAK

In the next few weeks, give yourself permission not to be perfect, and not to always do what you think someone wants you to do. Also, give yourself permission to tell people what **you** want some of the time. Of course, you will want to do this in a pleasant way, but be firm. For example, "I know you want me to pick you up after school, but I want to finish my shopping, so I can't do it today." Don't be afraid to say, "I want ..." You don't need to have excuses or good reasons for everything you want to do.

Every time you try letting yourself not be perfect, or telling someone what you want, take some time later in the day to briefly write down what happened. Write down how you felt, what the other person did or said, and how you feel about it now. At the end of each week look over what you have written.

Think about the consequences that have occurred as a result of your looking for less approval from others and from yourself. Were the results as bad as you thought they would be? Did other people manage to get along without you doing all those things? How do you feel about yourself? Do you feel more powerful, more in control of your life?

Most people find that if they try this for a while, they soon begin to enjoy feeling that they have a **choice**. They may even continue doing most of the things they were doing before, but now they are doing them because they have decided they want to, not because they feel they have to. This relieves a lot of the pressure they were feeling before. Also, they feel better about themselves because they find out that other people still like them — maybe even like them more — even though they aren't trying as hard to please them any more.

PEOPLE LEARNING TO NEED LESS APPROVAL

Here are two illustrations in which people discovered that giving up living their lives to win approval from others resulted in living much happier lives.

Barbara: Now I Choose For Myself

> My life has changed drastically since I've decided to be myself instead of the person I thought everyone wanted me to be. For years I was living what now seems like a false life. I took on society's implied attribution, "A good wife and mother tries to do everything perfectly," and turned it into an injunction, "Be a wife and mother who does everything perfectly." I was trying to be a model wife and mother in a model family according to what I thought as society's model.
>
> In order to try to live up to this false position, I performed my tasks at home and in the community almost to perfection; which, of course, meant not saying no when asked to do something for either my family or the community. I could only feel accepted if my behavior met the standards of other people. I did not feel worthwhile just for being myself, but only for my good behavior. ...
>
> The problem was that I had left myself no power of choice in my life. I let all my "shoulds" and other people's wants make my choice for me. Now I choose for myself. I look at the options available and make my own choices. I remind myself that I can't be everything to everyone; that feeling guilty about not meeting someone's expectations is a waste of energy.
>
> The way I feel about my relationships with other people now is as if I were saying to them: "I am Barbara, a person. I hope you will like me. If you choose not to, that's ok. I will survive because I like myself." Now I am excited about each day. Each day is a new beginning. I can enjoy the present moment. It is easier to accept others as they are. Most of all, I feel excited at discovering my ability to choose for myself. It's a great feeling.

James: I'm Proud of Who I Am

The black power movement has changed my outlook a lot and helped me feel proud of who I am instead of trying to be someone I'm not. When I was growing up as the oldest child in a black family, my parents taught me that to make it in the world as a black I had to be subservient, follow rules closely, and most important, I had to make it in school. Also, I had the additional responsibility of setting an example for my younger sisters and brothers.

It was a lot of pressure on me always having to do everything right, and excel, and I hated always being an example. In my high school there were about forty blacks in a school of over three hundred kids, so I was always conscious of the rules of the "white social structure." I also had absorbed my parents' belief that I had to do better than my white counterparts to be able to compete for a job, higher education, etc. ...

I was in college when the black power movement first began to reach me. It seemed to alter or change many of the values I had held for years. I started meeting blacks who no longer felt subservient, who expressed pride in being themselves and being black. They no longer felt they had to take a subservient position or conform to white values to get along. Instead of thinking of being black as a cross to bear, they replaced the burden with pride. ...

It took awhile before my values altered enough that I could stop seeing my own needs and desires as secondary to behaving appropriately. Slowly, I began to realize that I did not have to be submissive or sell my soul to purchase independence. I developed increased pride in myself. That's when I stopped going to school for my parents and started going for myself — and that's when I really started to like being there!

16

Change Your Life And Reduce Your Load By...........

Managing Your Time Wisely

Do you feel like you're always busy, yet just can't get everything done? Is your life full of half-finished projects? Do you have a mental list of things you'd really like to do if you could just find the time? Do you put off starting projects and then find you have to finish in a rush? A great deal of stress overload in people's lives is the result of time pressures like these.

DO YOU SEEM TO BE ALWAYS RUSHING?

Survey researchers and poll takers increasingly report that Americans complain of not having enough time. More than half of us say we feel rushed and often find ourselves thinking of all the things we need to do; 70% report not having time to get those things done. Modern technology is supposed to give us more time, and most of us use time-saving devices, but most of us still say that life is more hectic than it was five years ago. Even our free time is rushed. A recent survey of working mothers found that while 95% look forward to the weekend, 52% feel exhausted when it's over. More than 75% of American adults say they would like to have more time to spend with family or friends.

For example, consider Ruth's situation:

> As I looked at the stress in my life, I found that I was experiencing very high stress in my leisure time and my close relationships. I don't necessarily worry and feel guilty about my job when I am at home, but it seems like when I am off work there are always a million things I feel I should be doing around the house. I feel there isn't enough time when I am at home. I feel like I am always rushing.

> In fact, "rush" seems to be the key word in my life. The mornings before work are rushed trying to get two children up, dressed, fed, and ready for school and sitters. Two evenings a week are a rush leaving from work to get my daughter to ballet lessons. Other nights are a rush to get supper on with little evening left to relax.
>
> Unfortunately, when I feel rushed, I tend to lose my temper and raise my voice if someone in the family does something that displeases me. Then, I get upset about my reaction. I sometimes feel taken advantage of when I feel like I am not getting the help I need around the house.
>
> Most of the time I just feel like my system is on overload. There never seem to be enough hours in the day to accomplish all that needs to be done.

Some of Ruth's time problems, like most people's time problems, come from failing to set clear priorities. Most of us don't have an unlimited supply of time any more than we have an unlimited supply of money. Yet, we often act as though our time supply is unlimited. That is, we don't use our time **effectively**. Time management consultants tell us that the goal is not to use time efficiently (being constantly busy), it is to use time effectively (making the best use of our time).

THE KEY: CHOICE

The point is that making the **right choices** for yourself about how you'll use your time is what is important. When it comes to money, it is often easier to see that you must choose. If you only have $10.00, you can go to a movie, **or** you can buy a plant, **or** you can buy a new book, **or** you can go out for a couple of drinks. But you can't do **all** of these. You have to decide what would give you the most pleasure.

And, of course, this is assuming you don't **have to** spend the $10.00 to pay back a loan, buy food, or put a little gas in your car. If you have a pressing demand for the money, you will probably choose that as the best use for the $10.00 **at that time.** If not, you can choose another best use at that time. It is clear that you can only spend the $10.00 one way, and that after you spend it, it is gone. **It is the same for time**. If you have ten minutes, you have to choose the best way to spend it.

This doesn't mean you have to work all the time, or be super-organized, or worry about ever wasting a minute, or be always rushing to get more done. In fact, time management is just the opposite of these. It is a way of getting **more freedom**. This is true because time management involves taking a good look at what is important to **you** and seeing how you can use your time more effectively to get what you want done.

You may think you have very little choice or control over how you spend your time. Actually, you always have the choice. Of course, you have given up some of your freedom to decide how to spend your time in exchange for other things you consider important, like money, love, security, companionship, etc. — but ultimately, this was your choice too. Hopefully, your choices are designed to get you closer to your long-term goals.

USE YOUR TIME TO GET WHAT YOU WANT

Unfortunately people often **do not** use their time in ways that are directed toward their ultimate goals. For example, most people say they put a very high value on maintaining both excellent health and strong family relationships. Yet when questioned about the amount of time they **regularly** devote to pursuing these goals, many people admit it is very little. Most of us report that when we are short of time we will shortchange ourselves and our families rather than our jobs or our studies. We tell ourselves we'll make up for it later, but frequently when "later" comes, we're still too busy.

The problem usually is that people don't keep their long- term goals in mind. Many adults have either forgotten their goals or never clearly established them. We are going to provide you now with a way of looking at your long-term goals. After you have established these goals for yourself, we will show you how to begin managing your time so you can get what you really want out of life.

TEN STEPS TOWARD YOUR LONG-TERM GOALS

1. **Imagine**. Suppose you look up from this page and find standing in front of you a magic genie. "I am here to give you what you really want from life," says the genie, "even those things you secretly want but never thought you could get. So tell me what you want, and I will see that you get it."

2. **Wish**. What would you ask for? Remember you can make as many wishes as you want, and you should ask for even the things you think are impossible. Take a few minutes to think about this. Close your eyes and tell yourself what you **really** want.

3. **List.** Now, get a paper and pencil and make a list of all the things you decided to ask for. Be sure you write down what you really want, not just what seems easy to get. Don't forget to include goals that might seem frivolous like taking a "dream vacation," or learning to play an instrument.

4. **Consider**. As you have probably guessed by now, this list itemizes your real lifetime goals and **you** are the genie who can get them for yourself. But, of course, it will take more than a wave of a wand. You'll have to plan and set some priorities.

5. **Choose.** Next, you should look carefully at your list of wishes, selecting five that you want to begin to work on right now. Don't throw the rest of the list away. You can work on the others later.

6. **Target.** You will now need five more pieces of paper. At the top of each, write down one of your wishes. Write it down in a sentence that begins, "I want ...." For example, you might write, "I want to be in excellent health, with my body at its peak of fitness." Under that, write down how long you would like to give yourself to reach this goal — a year, five years, ten years, etc.

7. **Plan.** At this point you should have five papers, each of which has something you want written at the top, and your target date for achieving it written underneath. Now choose one of these papers. Under the amount of time you have given yourself to reach this goal, write down what you would like to have done toward it when half of the time has gone by. For example, if you want to reach your goal in five years, what do you want to have done toward the goal in two-and-a-half years? Then do the same for half of **that** time — for example, one-and-one-quarter years.

8. **Begin.** You can now see that you are getting closer to the present time in looking at your goal. So, it is time to look at what you can begin doing **right now** to be where you want to be in one, two, or five years. Make a list of things you could do in the **next month** to help you reach this goal. List as many things as you can think of, even though you know you don't have time to do them all.

9. **Promise.** You are now ready to decide how you want to begin working toward your goal. From the list of things you could do during the next month, decide on several that you are willing to **start on this week.** You don't have to finish them this week, but you must be willing to **start** on them this week. Write out your promises to yourself, beginning, "This week I will ....."

10. **Repeat.** You have now completed your list for this one goal. Repeat steps seven, eight, and nine for the goals you have on the other four papers.

A SAMPLE PLAN

Here is an example of how one of your papers should look when you have completed it:

GOAL: I want to be in excellent health, with my body at its peak of fitness.

TIME: I would like to reach this goal in **2 years**.

One year from now, I want to have lost 20 pounds, to have lowered my blood pressure by 10 points, to be getting no more headaches, and to be able to engage in vigorous physical activity for an hour at a time.

Six months from now, I want to be exercising regularly, I want to have lost 10 pounds, I want to be feeling more energetic, and I want to be getting no more than one headache a week.

ACTIVITIES: In the next month I could:

- Get a physical checkup
- Change my eating habits
- Read a book on aerobic exercise
- Go to an exercise class
- Start exercising regularly
- Try using techniques like relaxation or meditation to see if I get fewer headaches
- Watch less television so I have more time for physical activity
- Cut down the amount of coffee I drink to two cups a day or less

PROMISES: Next week I will:

- Call and make an appointment for a checkup
- Write down everything I eat and drink each day, including how much coffee I drink
- Get a book to read on aerobic exercise
- Decide what type of exercise I plan to do regularly
- Do a relaxation exercise once a day

Obviously, each week you will have to make a new list of activities you plan to do to get you closer to your goals. And as time goes on you will reach some of these goals or see them within reach and you will want to begin working on others. Keep changing your lists, continue to make promises to yourself and keep them, and you **will** each your goals.

FINDING TIME TO DO WHAT YOU WANT TO DO

By now you're probably saying, "I don't even have time to do all the things I have to do now, and you're asking me to do more things, plus take time every week to plan what I want to do — how is it possible?" Obviously, it isn't. You will have to give up some of the things you are doing now. But remember, it is **your goals** you will be working toward. So you will be substituting some of the things you **really** want to do for some things you don't want to do as much.

The main difference will be that you'll have to **think** about how you're spending your time and you'll have a plan. You'll have to decide which are the most important tasks to do each day and what can be left for another time. The easiest way to do this is to make a list each morning of what you want to do that day. Then number the activities in terms of how important they are to you. Then do the most important things first, or write down exactly when you will do them. If you don't get to everything, it will be the least important things that get left out.

Be sure to include having fun and relaxing on your list. Too often people leave **those** activities until last and then have no time for them. Some of the activities you rank as your highest priorities may be spending time with your spouse, children, or friends, going to a movie, or playing a game. (These activities may be very important to you if you have goals of improving your relationships with others or relaxing more.) You may find that activities like cleaning the house or washing the car are very low on your list and don't get done. That's ok. When you feel a real **need** to do those things, they will be higher on your list.

When you plan your days, look at the ways you spend your time and really ask yourself whether you **want** to use your time that way. For example, if you usually spend several hours each evening watching television, you may decide that you'd rather use that time to do something toward one of your goals. Whatever you decide, at least you will know that you are **choosing** the way you spend your time.

BENEFITS OF MANAGING YOUR TIME

When you begin managing your time this way, you will find that time pressure creates less stress for you. This is because you will know that you are in control of your time. You will know that you are using your time to get what you want in life and you will see that step by step you are getting closer to your goals. This feeling of **using** time, rather than feeling like there's never enough time, is an exhilarating change for most people.

Remember Ruth? She decided that one of her priorities was to have a more pleasant relationship with her family. She realized that to do that she needed a little "calm" time to herself each day. She talked to them about it and worked out a plan where she could have 20 uninterrupted minutes each evening for a relaxation or meditation exercise. She found that the relaxation time helped her deal more easily with situations and problems. Also, she felt more rested and much less irritable.

Ruth also started making lists of what she really needed to do each day and then what she would like to do, but could put off. She realized that some of the tasks she thought she always **had to get done** in the morning could be left undone without dire consequences. She even managed to leave her bed unmade in the morning if she was in a hurry. Ruth also found other advantages to the lists. They saved her energy since she no longer needed to continually run through mental lists trying to remember what needed to be done, and made it easier for her to say "no" to extra requests that could be refused, since she clearly didn't have the time.

Ruth is still working on this area, but reports benefits already:

> Changing habits takes time. I still get uptight about my house being a mess if someone is coming over. But most of the time I feel much less urgency about my time. Because I complete the tasks on my list, I feel ok about taking free (guilt free) time for myself in the evenings and on weekends. It's wonderful to have some time when I don't have anything I **have** to do. In the last six weeks I have been able to see a couple of friends, luxuriate in a bubble bath or two, write some letters to old friends and family, and read a book I'd been saving since Christmas. Being able to enjoy myself and still feel that I am accomplishing goal- oriented tasks is an amazing feeling.

17

Change Your Life And Reduce Your Load By...........

Being Nice To Yourself

Taking care of yourself is important. If you find time in your life to do things that give you pleasure, you will be a more relaxed, happier person.

LEARNING TO GIVE TO YOURSELF

Frequently people don't do nice things for themselves because they think it would be selfish or are afraid someone else will think they are selfish. If you feel this way, remind yourself that one of the greatest gifts you can give another person is to be a cheerful person yourself. So, you need to spend some time regularly keeping yourself happy.

You may feel more comfortable giving yourself treats if you think of them as rewards. You can plan to give yourself a reward after you have completed a job you've been putting off, or when you've done some specific work toward one of your goals, or after you get through a hard day.

On the other hand, you can decide to have fun just because you want to. Or you can do it because you know that having some play in your life makes living more relaxing and rewarding. In fact, some research shows that playing actively and joyfully has some of the benefits of meditation. It alleviates many of the physiological effects of stress and tension, and leaves you feeling calm, energetic, and content.

Some people are so used to being responsible and serious that they find it difficult to play and have fun. They feel anxious about "wasting time," or awkward and embarrassed participating in activities that have no obvious productive outcome. If you are this way, have patience with these feelings and push yourself to gradually take more time to relax.

In a sense, this is the essence of everything we've talked about in this book. Taking the time for yourself to do relaxation exercises, meditate, exercise, use imagery or expand your awareness of your surroundings are all ways of being nice to yourself. If you find this difficult, remind yourself of two very important points:

1) You have the **right** to take time for yourself.

2) You have the **right** to be at least as nice to yourself as you are to other people.

TAKING CARE OF YOURSELF HELPS OTHERS

Not only can you see the two points as rights, you can see them as obligations. Remember what we've said about how stress can lead to illness. You aren't doing anyone any favors if you work yourself so hard that you get sick. You wouldn't take a nice new car and just run it all the time with no maintenance or even an oil change. So why do it to yourself? If a doctor told you that it was essential for your health that you take a certain amount of time each day or week for yourself, you would very likely do it — and without feeling guilty. So save yourself the doctor's bill, give yourself a break, and find some time for yourself.

This point is especially important for those people who are spending a lot of their time taking care of someone else — perhaps a young child, a frail aged parent, or a sick or disabled family member. While you may feel that you **should** give all your energy to your caregiving tasks and always put the other person's needs ahead of your own, this is a shortsighted view. You **must** take time for yourself so that you can maintain the health and energy you need to continue to take care of your loved one.

BENEFITS OF FUN

When you try being nice to yourself this way, you may be amazed at how much relief you feel from the emotional exhaustion and stress of daily life. Here are a few people's accounts of the difference taking time for fun has made in their lives:

> "I feel like a dam has been opened in me, which had been closed off and which made it hard for me to feel or enjoy life. This is very freeing for me — I feel more positive about myself and about life."

"Now that I freely give myself the time, even such a simple thing as reading the Sunday paper in quiet and relaxation is a great pleasure!"

"My husband and I made a deal. We each take one evening a week to do just what we want, while the other one spends time with the kids. Since we both work, we don't have much free time, and I really look forward to and enjoy that time to myself—and I always use it to do something I want to do—not something I should do, just something I feel like doing."

"It seems as though a whole era in my life has ended. All this newness is amazing and very awesome. I really believe I deserve the luxury of taking time off just for fun, and now that I'm doing it, I'd never go back to living the way I was before."

HOW TO BEGIN

Ask yourself how much play and fun you have in your life. Then make a list of as many things as you can think of that you really enjoy doing. Include activities you once enjoyed, but haven't done for awhile. Then add to your list ideas you've had about things you think would be fun to do, but you haven't tried yet. To get you started, we'll make a short sample list.

- Crafts, like macrame or woodworking
- Dancing
- Playing an instrument
- Reading the newspaper or magazines
- Singing
- Visiting friends
- Sports, like tennis, racquetball, or swimming
- Taking long walks
- Writing poems or stories
- Spending some time alone, just thinking.
- Taking your kids on a picnic or to a ballgame
- Cooking a new or favorite dish
- Having a party or going to one
- Drawing or painting
- Acting in a play
- Going out to eat or to a movie

The possibilities are endless. You will probably find that you remember many things you once enjoyed but have forgotten about for years. Try these activities again. It doesn't matter how good you are at them — fun is the goal. You will find that you feel younger and more alive, as well as more relaxed, as you begin to add more enjoyment to your life. Looking forward to a pleasant activity you have planned for the evening can make the whole day seem brighter.

ADD FUN TO YOUR PLANS

Planning for fun is just as important as any other planning. Now that you have your list of activities you enjoy, or think you might enjoy, make specific plans for adding some of these to your life. Does your community have clubs or classes you could join? Can you organize a group of friends to work on a craft or play a sport together regularly?

Can you arrange with your family to have some time for yourself when they agree not to interrupt you? (Even young children can be taught to respect the privacy of others if this is explained to them and they know you still have time for them.) Can you make an agreement with your spouse or a friend to try some new activities together in your free time?

Watch out for over-planning, though. If you have a tendency to be competitive, you may easily slip into straining to excel in your leisure time too. The free time activities you choose should be just that — free. If you're a golfer or tennis player always trying to improve your game, these activities probably aren't very relaxing for you, so you'll still need some time out for less serious pursuits.

When you begin actively thinking about adding more fun to your life you will find yourself coming up with lots of ideas. The secrets are believing you deserve it and planning for it so you know you'll get it. Don't just leave it to chance or you will find your old habits of flopping in front of the television or filling all your time with miscellaneous tasks. Decide to be **actively** nice to yourself. You certainly deserve it!

AN EXAMPLE

Ted started this project to add some fun to his life at the same time he began an exercise program. He wanted, in his words, to lower his "boiling point," and to feel less frustration in his daily life. Choosing to add play to his life along with exercise was a good choice for Ted because his competitive nature easily carried over into his exercise program. So, while it gave him physical release, he still needed another type of relaxation.

Ted: Soothing Effects of Music

I knew my habits were conducive to stress and that I had never learned to deal with it in the past. I decided I was a very serious, hard-working person. I started this stress-management project with much interest as I was determined to learn to relax. One reason I decided to make finding time for fun a part of my plan was that my brother had been telling me I work all the time and I was beginning to think he was right.

I enjoy music and have a large library of albums, but I usually don't take time to really listen to them. Mostly when I put on some music, I'm doing something else at the same time, so I'm only hearing it "with one ear."

I decided to spend a few hours each week playing my records and getting started on a project I'd been thinking about for a long time — making tapes grouping together songs I particularly like around certain themes. I couldn't wait to get started! ...

Once I really decided to give myself time for the music, it wasn't as hard as it had always seemed it would be to find the time. I guess it was really just a matter of feeling ok about doing something just for fun.

During the first week I didn't notice any great changes in the way I felt, but I did feel good about doing something for myself. Before, I thought that all that was required of an adult was to tend to responsibilities and life would go on. Taking time out, I began to realize that I needed something more to truly find happiness. ...

I think I had been running along so hard and fast for so long that I had really forgotten how I used to feel when I had more time to relax. It's almost as if I had lost touch with the person I used to be. ...

As the weeks went along, I came to enjoy my music project more and more. My wife (who at first seemed to think the whole thing was a waste of time) listened to some of my tapes and liked them. We began coming up with ideas together for more tapes. We made a special one for my brother's birthday last week and he loved it. ...

I'm still keeping this as just a fun activity, though. I'm not getting into deadlines for getting tapes done or being an absolute perfectionist about doing them in certain ways the way I do with most areas of my life. My only criteria for this is that I enjoy it. ...

I think doing this has made me more aware of myself and somehow more sensitive to other people too. I've slowed down some and no longer try to solve all situations by full frontal assault. This has positive effects for my business as well as for me as a person.

I have also noticed that I am somewhat calmer in most stressful or disappointing situations. An excellent example is the way I coped with my favorite team's ups and downs during the World Series. My wife couldn't believe that I didn't yell, scream, curse, and throw things following the tragic conclusion to the second game. Frankly, neither could I.

SECTION IV : A QUESTION OF CHOICE

18. DO YOU WANT TO KEEP ON STRUGGLING WITH THAT HEAVY LOAD ....
    OR CHOOSE TO MAKE SOME CHANGES?

18

Do You Want To Keep On Struggling With That Heavy Load...........

Or Choose To Make Some Changes?

We now come to the end of **our** work on dealing with your stress overload and the beginning of **your** work on this problem. We have presented the techniques; you have read them and probably experimented with some. Now you are ready to begin putting these procedures to work in your life to get relief from the tension and pressure you have been experiencing.

THERE ARE NO INSTANT CURES!

Remember, in the beginning of this book we told you that although these techniques are easy to learn, it is not easy to change your habits and ways of dealing with stress. If it were easy, stress would not be the tremendous problem it is for people today. Most of us are looking for an instant cure — just like we would all like a harmless magic pill that would make us lose twenty pounds while still eating all our favorite foods.

Even though we want to change, most of us have very little patience with ourselves as we go about it. We tend to make grand (often unrealistic) resolutions, and then as soon as we slip a little bit, we decide we just "can't do it," and return to our old ways. It is important to realize that change takes time, that we will have occasional relapses, and that we can learn from these slips. Here are some tricks to help you when you're having a hard time changing your habits:

- **Find a replacement for a habit you want to change.** If you want to cut down on caffeine, replace it with a non-caffeinated drink. If you want to stop responding to people in anger, find a reason to leave the room for a brief break before you react.

- **Make realistic plans.** Don't try to change your entire life in the first week. Setting unrealistically high goals can lead to quick feelings of failure.

- **Avoid "all-or-nothing thinking."** When you slip, think of it as a mistake, not a failure. Learn from the experience by looking at what circumstances, people or emotions triggered the difficulty.

- **Reward yourself for positive behavior.** Set up situations to encourage yourself to stick to your resolves. Decide to read the paper **after** you exercise, or watch a movie **after** you meditate.

- **Expect the best for yourself.** Don't give yourself negative messages like, "I never could stick to anything," or make excuses like, "I'm too busy to change right now." Keep telling yourself you can succeed if you make realistic plans and have patience with yourself.

DECIDE TO MAKE CHANGES

The techniques we have presented work. We know this because we use them ourselves and have taught them to many, many people. These techniques are effective in reducing stress overload. As we said in the beginning, there is only one condition you must meet to make these techniques work for you. You must **decide to put forth the energy to change your life.** You can do it, and when you do you will find the payoff is well worth the effort.

Let's review the techniques we have discussed. We have classified the techniques into two groups:

1. Techniques that make you feel better and make your load easier to carry:

(1) Relaxing your muscles
(2) Meditating
(3) Doing mantra
(4) Exercising regularly
(5) Eating for good health
(6) Expanding your awareness
(7) Using fantasy

2. Techniques that help you change the way you live so that you reduce the load you are carrying:

(1) Looking at the world differently
(2) Putting yourself in someone else's shoes
(3) Giving up being right
(4) Learning to deal with criticism
(5) Needing less approval from others
(6) Managing your time wisely
(7) Being nice to yourself

CREATE YOUR PERSONAL PLAN

As we have said, while all these techniques are effective for some people, **you** are the best judge of what will work for you. At this point, you will find it useful to re-read the first three chapters and look again at your Stress Profile or your answers to the questions in Chapter Two (which helped you look at the levels and patterns of stress in your life). This will help you decide which of the methods will be most useful in meeting your needs. Review the techniques. If there are some you skipped over, or if you haven't tried some of the activities presented, go back and try these at least once.

You are now ready to decide on your own individual stress management plan. **The plan you make now should be a plan for the next six weeks, and you should absolutely promise yourself that you will stick to your plan for six weeks, no matter what.** This is very important because it is necessary to use these techniques regularly for a while before you can evaluate the results.

At the end of six weeks you should sit down and go through the questions in Chapter Two again to look at your stress level. Decide whether you want to simply continue with the techniques from your original plan or continue these and add some new techniques, or change your original plan and try some different techniques.

Again, make a plan for six weeks and stick to it. After you have done this for several six-week periods, you will have a much better idea of what works for you and some of the techniques will have become so much a part of your life that you won't want to give them up.

Remember, the most important thing is that you stick to what you decide for the **entire six weeks**! You get essentially no benefit from trying one technique for a few days and then another for a few days. To let these techniques work for you, you must change your old habits and develop new ones — and that takes time!

Obviously, you must create your own plan to meet your individual needs and to suit your lifestyle. We will provide you with some suggestions and a sample plan to get you started. You can go on from there.

SIX SERIOUS SUGGESTIONS

1. **Begin by making a commitment to use at least two techniques on a regular basis.**

2. **Choose one technique from the first group** — "Techniques which make you feel better and make your load easier to carry." Promise yourself you will take time to do it at least five days each week. For example, meditate five days each week, or exercise at least five days each week, or write down what you eat and follow the instructions for improving your diet, etc.

3. **Choose one technique from the second group** — "Techniques which help you change the way you live so that you reduce the load you are carrying." Promise yourself that during the first week of your plan you will reread the section on that technique several times and go through the exercises we have provided. Then, in the next five weeks find as many opportunities as you can to use this technique in your life. Get a notebook and write down your progress as you go along.

4. **If you have time, select a book that interests you** from the list of recommended readings at the end of this book, and promise yourself you will read it during the six-week period.

5. **When you have extra time, read** over a section on one of the techniques you are not using in your plan and experiment with it. Think about including it in your next six-week plan.

6. **Tell yourself that this may look like a lot of work, but that you are worth it!** It's about time you did something for you, and you're going to make these changes because you want to do this for yourself.

SAMPLE PLAN

Here is an example of what a six-week plan would look like, following the suggestions above.

For the next six weeks, I will:

1) Set aside twenty minutes each day to **meditate** (either when I get home from work or at my lunch hour)

2) Work on **giving up being right** and keep track in a notebook of how this is working for me every day.

3) Read one of the books on physical exercise and investigate exercise classes and health clubs close to where I live.

4) When I have extra time, I will read over the sections on **imagery, expanding awareness,** or **being nice to yourself,** and try out some of these techniques.

A PLAN IN ACTION

Janice was feeling a lot of stress as a full-time teacher, a graduate student, and a wife when she began her stress-management project as part of a class assignment. This is the report she wrote two months later:

Janice: Eight Weeks of Change

Initially I was somewhat skeptical about making this stress-management plan. My concern was finding the time to include another task in an already hectic schedule. I looked at the options available and chose deep muscle relaxation, combined with the ideas of putting yourself in another's shoes and managing time wisely.

I did the deep muscle relaxation five times a week (Tuesday, Thursday, Friday, Saturday and Sunday). During the work week I did it as soon as I got home from work because I was alone and would not be disturbed or distracted. On weekends I used the technique at varying times, usually when I was alone and in the later part of the day. So far I have been doing this for nine weeks. ...

I used "putting myself in another's shoes" in several personal situations that were upsetting to me. I used the procedure before I discussed the situation with the other person involved.

"I used the time management practices in an ongoing way. I did the initial goal setting eight weeks ago. Each Friday afternoon I noted my accomplishments by checking them off the list (a great reinforcer!), and then made a new list. I added items to my calendar on a daily, realistic basis. I focused on three main goals: completing my professional studies successfully, improving my relationship with my husband, and having more free (guiltless) time.

As I consider the changes in my behavior and level of stress during the last two months, I find that some changes relate to a particular technique and some to a combination of two or more methods.

First, I have reduced my smoking over the past two months from 1-1/2 packs of cigarettes a day to less than 1/2 pack per day. I think that doing the deep muscle relaxing has reduced my need for cigarettes after a "hard" day. Smoking after the relaxation just seems to tense me up again and start my heart pounding. ...

Another behavior that I have changed is my frequency of drinking alcohol. In the past I would come home and have a couple of beers to help me unwind approximately four times per week. Usually I would then lose all motivation to do anything constructive. I wasn't relaxed; I was sedated!

Since I now come home and use deep muscle relaxing right away, I am unwound but have the motivation to do household tasks, cook dinner, etc. The drinking was an example of maladaptive coping which actually resulted in additional stress because I would feel guilty about those tasks which were not completed. Even a clean house can be a source or reinforcement — pride in a job well done and compliments and appreciation from others. ...

I also suffer from classic migraine headaches. I have had only one migraine headache since I began using the techniques to reduce stress. That particular headache was of less intensity than most others I have experienced. Once when I began to get the warning signs of a headache (blind spots in vision, numbness in fingers), I immediately took two Tylenol caplets and then did the deep muscle relaxation. In the past, the Tylenol has not prevented a headache. This time the headache was minor — I only felt pain when I moved my head quickly — and I wasn't incapacitated in any way. ...

Another change I noticed recently is that on the days I use the deep muscle relaxation, I seem to sleep better. I fall asleep more quickly and wake up feeling more refreshed. This could also be related to managing my time more wisely because I'm not worried about tasks not accomplished. ...

Because I focused on a few specific goals and devised both long and short term timelines, I have organized my days far more constructively. For the last two months I have been able to remain current in the weekly reading assignments for my classes, which reduces my stress a lot. When an exam nears, I can simply review already familiar material as opposed to my previous practice of reading and studying information at the same time. I have also found that I have more free time for myself in the evenings.

Over the last six weeks my experience with and opinion of the deep muscle relaxation has undergone some changes. I was skeptical about the value of using the technique. It took about 35 minutes each time I did the process during the first two weeks. Since then, that has decreased to about 20 minutes per session. I now look forward to the relaxation.

I have also begun to recognize my personal physical indicators of stress. Usually my shoulders tighten and my neck gets stiff. At other times, I get a sick empty feeling in the pit of my stomach. When I am at home and I notice these indicators, I can use the deep muscle relaxing technique to get relief. ...

Just recently, I have begun to use the technique on the job. The junior high students I work with are in a special program because of their inappropriate behavior. Often they are very angry, argumentative and surly. When I start feeling my stress level rising now, I'll go back to my desk and use the relaxation procedure. The positive result is that I become more relaxed, feel more pleasant, and seem to be less likely to use an authoritarian approach with the student. And while I've been "relaxing," the youth has had time to cool down. Interactions at this point seem far more constructive.

I have also practiced taking the perspective of the kids at school. Most of them seem to expect to be dealt with in an authoritarian way. By putting myself in their shoes and remembering how I felt at their age, I have been able to discuss issues with them calmly. It seems to decrease my judgemental thoughts and statements, help me to praise their accomplishments, and give me ways of pointing out to them the benefits of changing their behavior. They seem less defensive and hostile, and our interactions are more pleasant. ...

One change that my husband has noticed is that I haven't seemed to snap at him as frequently or jump to conclusions prematurely. He also feels that I have brought up issues in our relationship more constructively. Because I am more relaxed in my approach to these issues and seem to more clearly understand or empathize with his situation or point of view, he says he feels like I care more about him. In other words, by putting myself in his shoes before a discussion of a problem, I can see beyond my own position.

Overall, I feel much better about myself these days. When I do think something unfavorable about myself, I focus on my behavior rather than labelling myself negatively. The value of these techniques seems to be limitless. Practicing the stress-management procedures has truly added to my personal enjoyment and quality of life. I plan to continue and hope to experience continuous levels and stages of growth.

BEGIN TODAY!

By now you should have made your own plan and be well on your way to a happier, more relaxed life. Whenever you find yourself getting discouraged, or feeling that you're too busy to stick to your plan, remind yourself that you owe it to yourself and the people around you to do what you need to do to prevent feeling overloaded by pressure and stress.

When you are tense and anxious, not only do you feel miserable, but you spread this misery around to other people you contact. On the other hand, when you feel alive, joyful, and energetic, you spread those feelings to the people around you. Let's unite in a campaign to wipe out tension in the world and spread joy everywhere, beginning with ourselves!

RECOMMENDED READING LIST

LIFE-STRESS & STRESS MANAGEMENT

Friedman, M. & Roseman, R.H. *Type A Behavior and Your Heart*. (Fawcett, 1974).
Gould, R. *Transformations*. (Simon and Schuster, 1978).
Lazarus, R. & Folkman, S. *Stress, Appraisal and Coping*. (Springer, 1984).
Hepworth, M. and Featherstone, M. *Surviving Middle Age* . (Basil Blackwell, 1982).
Monat, A. & Lazarus, R. *Stress and Coping: An Anthology*. (Columbia University Press, 1985).
Ruben, H. *Super Marriage: Overcoming the Predictable Crises of Married Life*. (Bantam, 1986).
Scarf, M. *Unfinished Business: Pressure Points In the Lives of Women*. (Ballantine, 1980).
Selye, H. *Stress Without Distress*. (Lippincott, 1974).
Sheehy, G. *Passages*. (Dutton, 1974)
Sheehy, G. *Pathfinders*. (Bantam, 1982)
Viorst, J. *Necessary Losses*. (Ballantine, 1987).
Woolfolk, R. & Lehrer, P. *Principles and Practice of Stress Management*. (Guilford Press, 1984).

RELAXATION, MEDITATION, & MANTRA

Benson, H. *Beyond the Relaxation Response*. (Berkley Books, 1985).
Benson, H. *The Relaxation Response*. (Avon, 1975).
Blofeld, J. *Mantras: Sacred Words of Power*. (Dutton, 1977).
Carrington, P. *Freedom in Meditation*. (Anchor, 1977).
Easwaran, E. *The Mantram Handbook*. (Nilgiri Press, 1977).
Gendlin, E. *Focusing*. (Bantam, revised edition, 1981).

Golas, T. *The Lazy Man's Guide to Enlightenment.* (Seed Center, 1971).

Goldstein, J. & Kornfield, J. *Seeking the Heart of Wisdom.* (Shambhala Publications, 1987).

LeShan, L. *How to Meditate.* (Bantam, 1974).

Mouradian, K. *Reflective Meditation: A Mind Calming Technique.* (A Quest Book, 1982).

Shapiro, D. *Precision Nirvana.* (Prentice-Hall, 1978).

Stroebel, C.F. *QR: The Quieting Reflex.* (Berkley, 1982).

EXERCISE & DIET

Bicycling Magazine's Fitness Through Cycling. (Rodale Press, 1985).

Brody, J. *Jane Brody's Good Food Book: Living the High Carbohydrate Way.* (W.W. Norton, 1985).

Christensen, A. *The American Yoga Association: Beginner's Manual.* (Simon & Schuster, 1987).

Cooper, K.H. *The Aerobics Way.* (Bantam, 1978).

Cooper, K.H. *The New Aerobics.* (Bantam, 1970).

Fonda, J. *Jane Fonda's New Workout and Weight Loss Program.* (Simon and Schuster, 1986).

Goor, R. and Goor, N. *Eater's Choice: A Food Lover's Guide to Lower Cholesterol.* (Houghton Mifflin, 1987).

Hittleman, R. *Richard Hittleman's Yoga: 28 day Exercise Plan.* (Bantam, 1969).

Millman, D. *The Warrior Athlete: Body, Mind and Spirit Self Transformation Through Total Training.* (Stillpaint Publishing, 1979).

Rowan, R.L. *How To Control High Blood Pressure Without Drugs.* (Ballantine, 1986).

Sweetgall, R., Rippe, J. & Katch, F. *Rockport's Fitness Walking.* (Putnam Publishing Group, 1985).

Vaz, K. and Zempel, C. *Swim Swim: A Complete Handbook for Fitness Swimmers.* (Contemporary Books, 1986).

Wurtman, J.J. *Managing Your Mind and Mood Through Food.* (Harper and Row, 1986).

Yetiv, J.Z. *Popular Nutritional Practices: Sense and Nonsense.* (Dell, 1988).

EXPANDING AWARENESS & FANTASY

Bry, A. *Visualization: Directing the Movies of Your Mind.* (Barnes and Noble, 1979).
Gawain, Shakti. *Creative Visualization.* (Bantam, 1982).
Huxley, L.A. *You Are Not the Target.* (Jeremy Tarcher, 1986).
Johnson, S. *One Minute for Myself: How To Manage Your Most Valuable Asset.* (Avon Books, 1985).
LeBoeuf, M. *Imageering: How To Profit From Your Creative Powers.* (McGraw Hill Paperbacks, 1982).
Nhat Hanh, Thich. *The Miracle of Mindfulness.* (Beacon, 1976).
Stevens, J. *Awareness.* (Bantam, 1971).

ATTITUDE CHANGE, CRITICISM, & APPROVAL

Alberti, R. and Emmons, M. *Your Perfect Right.* (Impact Publishers, 4th edition, 1982).
Bach, R. *Illusions.* (Dell, 1979).
Burns, D.D. *Feeling Good: The New Mood Therapy.* (Signet, 1980).
DeRosis, H. & Pelligrino, V. *The Book of Hope: How Women Can Overcome Depression.* (Bantam, 1976).
Dyer, W.D. *Pulling Your Own Strings.* (Avon, 1978).
Dyer, W.D. *Your Erroneous Zones.* (Avon, 1976).
Emery, G. *Own Your Own Life.* (Signet, 1982).
Hyatt, C. and Gottlieb, L. *Where Smart People Fail: Rebuilding Yourself for Success.* (Penguin Books, 1987).
Kaufman, B.N. *To Love Is to Be Happy With.* (Fawcett, 1977).
Kopp, S. *Mirror, Mask and Shadow: The Risks and Rewards of Self-Acceptance.* (Bantam, 1982).
Lerner, H.G. *The Dance of Anger.* (Perennial Library, Harper & Row, 1985).
Matke, P.H.C. *Selective Awareness.* (Prima Publishing and Communications, 1987).
Miller, S., Wackman, D., Nunnally, E., & Saline, C. *Straight Talk.* (Signet, 1981).
Prather, H. *Notes to Myself: My Struggle to Become a Person.* (Bantam, 1970).
Rogers, C. & Stevens, B. *Person to Person.* (Pocket Books, 1971).
Rubin, T. *Reconciliations: Inner Peace in an Age of Anxiety.* (Berkley Books, 1982).

Smith, M.J. *When I Say No, I Feel Guilty*. (Bantam, 1975).

TIME MANAGEMENT

Koberg, D. & Bagnall, J. *The Universal Traveler: A Soft-Systems Guide to Creativity, Problem Solving, and the Process of Reaching Goals*. (William Kaufmann, 1972).
Lakein, A. *How to Get Control of Your Time and Your Life*. (Signet, 1973).
Scott, D. *How to Put More Time in Your Life* (Signet, 1981).
Sher, B. *Wishcraft: How to Get What You Really Want*. (Ballantine, 1979).

A NOTE ABOUT

THE

COMPUTERIZED STRESS INVENTORY

Ten years ago we were teaching stress management skills in employee seminars and community workshops. We found that people wanted to learn more about their own stress, and less about the general principles of stress. After an exhaustive search for a test that would give people a detailed, personal report describing their stress, we began creating our own.That test eventually became our *Comprehensive Computerized Stress Inventory* , which **gives people an accurate, easy-to-understand picture of their personal stress patterns.**

Since 1984 (when we finally had our test ready to use), thousands of people have completed our *Comprehensive Computerized Stress Inventory* questionnaire in their doctor, psychologist, or counselor's office, wellness center, or corporate fitness program. The professionals have people answer the questions at a computer, or on a written questionnaire. Then, using our computer program, they process the answers and print out individual *Stress Profiles* , which describe each person's high stress areas and areas of strength. The *Stress Profile* also suggests specific chapters in this book to read for help with each high stress area.

If you would like to take the *Computerized Stress Inventory*, but don't know where to find it in your area, write to us, using the form on the next page, and we will let you know how you can most easily take the test. (If the form has already been removed from this book, write to us: Preventive Measures, Inc., 1115 West Campus Road, Lawrence, KS 66044; or call (913) 842-5078.

MAIL THIS FORM TO:

Preventive Measures, Inc.
1115 West Campus Road
Lawrence, KS 66044
Phone: (913) 842-5078

- - ✂ -

☐ Please let me know how I can most easily take the *Preventive Measures' Computerized Stress Inventory* in my area and get my personal *Stress Profile* .

Name____

(Please print)

Address______________________________________

City____________________ State_____ Zip _________

Nearest Large City______________________________

☐ I am interested in discount prices for ordering extra copies of this book. Please send me your price list for quantity orders.